Poverty and Social Developments in Peru, 1994–1997

The World Bank
Washington, D.C.

ISSN: 0253-2123

Library of Congress Cataloging-in-Publication Data has been applied for.

CONTENTS

BASIC INDICATORS TABLE

General

Area, land[1]	sq km, thousands	1,280
Population, 1996[1]	millions	24.2
growth rate, 1980-1996[1]	percent per annum	2.1
density, 1996[1]	per sq km	18.7

Social Indicators

malnutrition, chronic, 1997[2]	percent of children below five years	23.8
infant mortality, 1996[1]	per 1000 live births	42.0
under-five mortality, 1996[1]	per 1000	58.0
adolescent fertility rate, 1995[1]	birth per 1,000 women age 15-19	52.0
total fertility rate, 1996[1]	births per women	3.1
life expectancy at birth, 1996[1]	years	68.0
literacy rate, 1997[2]	population age 6 and over	90.2
net enrollment rates		
urban primary[2]	percent of relevant age group	90.0
rural primary[2]	percent of relevant age group	88.0
urban secondary[2]	percent of relevant age group	78.0
rural secondary[2]	percent of relevant age group	49.0
poverty incidence, 1997[2]	percent	49.0
poverty gap, 1997[2]	percent	16.0
severe poverty incidence, 1997[2]	percent	14.8
income inequality, total, 1997[2]	Gini coefficient	.484
child labor, 1997[2]	percent of children, age 6 to 14, working more than 15 hrs per week	11.8
electricity connections, 1997[2]	percent of population	73.7
sanitation connections , 1997[2]	percent of population	58.6
water, public net, 1997[2]	percent of population	72.8

Economic Indicators

GNP per capita, 1998[3]	$US	2,497
GDP growth, 1998[3]	percent	0.70
Inflation, 1998[3]	percent (end of period)	6.01
budget balance, 1998[3]	consolidated NFPS as % of GDP	-0.6
current account, 1998[3]	percent of GDP	-6.0

---

[1]   World Bank (1998), *World Development Indicators*, Washington D.C.

[2]   Staff estimates based on Instituto Cuánto (1997), *Encuesta Nacional de Hogares sobre Medición de Niveles de Vida*, Lima.

[3]   World Bank estimates based on data from Central Bank of Peru.

Currency Equivalents
Currency Unit – Nuevo Sol

US$1.00 = 3.33 soles (March 31, 1999)

Government FISCAL YEAR
January 1 to December 31

Acronyms and Abbreviations

BanMat	Banco de Materiales
CIAS	Consejo Interministerial de Asuntos Sociales
COOPOP	Oficina de Cooperación Popular
ENACE	Empresa Nacional de Edificaciones
ENAHO	Encuesta Nacional de Hogares
ENHOVI	Encuesta de Hogares sobre Violencia
ENNIV	Encuesta Nacional de Hogares sobre Medición de Niveles de Vida
FONAVI	Fondo Nacional de Vivienda
FONCODES	Fondo Nacional de Compensación y Desarrollo Social
GRADE	Grupo de Análisis para el Desarrollo
IDB	Inter-American Development Bank
INABIF	Instituto Nacional de Bienestar Familiar
INEI	Instituto Nacional de Estadística e Informática
IMF	International Monetary Fund
INFES	Infraestructura Nacional Para Educación y Salud
IPSS	Instituto Peruano de Seguridad Social
LSMS	Living Standard Measurement Survey
MECOVI	Programa para el Mejoramiento de las Encuestas y la Medición de las Condiciones de Vida
PACFO	Programa de Complementación Alimentaria para Grupos en Mayor Riesgo
PAR	Proyecto de Apoyo al Reboplamiento y Desarrollo de Zonas de Emergencia
PRONAA	Programa Nacional de Asistencia Alimentaria
USAID	United States Agency for International Development
Ute-FONAVI	Unidad Técnica – Fondo Nacional de Vivienda

ABSTRACT

This report evaluates social progress in Peru from 1994 to 1997. It carries mainly good news but also reports several worrisome developments. The good news is that social welfare improved over the three years - and this is true when looked at from a variety of angles. The poverty rate declined by several percentage points and stood at 49 percent in 1997. Severe poverty also declined, from about 19 to 15 percent. School attendance rose slightly, literacy rates increased from 87 to 90 percent, and the population is healthier. Most important among the latter, the rate of malnutrition for children below the age of five further dropped. These improvements are without doubt due to the favorable overall economic environment, with per capita real growth rates from 1994 to 1997 at about 3.5 percent. We estimate that about 1.3 million additional jobs were created in the economy, absorbing both a population increase and a higher participation rate in the labor force. Many of these new jobs are informal jobs, however, so workers are without formal contracts, pension insurance, or health insurance. Informality in Peru remains at a constant rate of about 45 percent of urban employment, even higher in rural areas.

But there are also some worrisome developments to report - and most of them are closely knit together. Economic growth and Government programs have not been spread equally and have not benefited everybody. First, regional disparities have grown, with some regions showing enormous progress, especially Lima, and other regions falling relatively behind, especially the rural areas in the highlands. This different regional development is also mirrored in the distribution of major public investments: While the government has made an effort to reach out more to the marginal rural population, this effort has only partially translated into measurable benefits. Of the large achievements in education, health and infrastructure, about 70 percent have been in cities. In international comparisons Peru remains one of the countries with an extremely high variation of regional income.

Second, with regional disparities increasing we also find some evidence that inequality has risen in the three years under study - a small increase in inequality can be observed when using several measurement methods and when looking at the distribution of income or wealth alike.

Third, Peru's development in the past years has been inclusive for many but exclusive for others. While we find gender differences narrowing and vulnerable groups such as migrants and the landless sharing the benefits of development, certain groups appear to have fallen further behind or remain highly at risk of deprivation. One group is clearly the indigenous population. Their social and political integration is still far from achieved. Similarly, the social situation of children remains bleak.

A number of factors have influenced household welfare over time, in both positive and negative ways. First, surprisingly, households were more likely to advance if their income stemmed from the informal sector than from the formal sector. This is true in urban areas as well as in informal off-farm employment in rural areas. Second, household size matters. Larger families have done worse than smaller ones – this relationship can work through higher dependency ratios that can limit the ability of households to save. Third, more education means faster advancement. Finally, savings and access to basic services like water, electricity or sanitation is not only of immediate support to households but helps them advance faster in ways not just directly connected to services access. We also find that bundling of such services matters: providing two services jointly has a more positive effect than the sum of providing each one separately.

On face value, Peru's growth path over the past years was pro-poor because the sectors where workers and their dependents are most likely to be poor (construction, commerce and agriculture) grew fastest. This appears to have helped the poor in construction and commerce. In agriculture, however, poverty reduction was slower than could have been hoped for. Employment creation as a corollary to agricultural growth was not strong. This could be due to a productivity backlog stemming from the recession at the beginning of the 1990s, implying that agricultural growth first led to more intensive work, i.e. longer hours per employed person.

A number of simulations show how important growth remains for poverty reduction in Peru. The simulations do show, however, that the type of growth and its regional distribution will matter - the more growth is based in agriculture, construction and commerce, and the more its impacts filter through to the rural highlands and lowlands, the more poverty will be reduced in the short run. While the growth pattern should not be artificially tilted towards such sectors, investment in these sectors will depend on a continuation of non-discrimination policies.

The distribution of social and anti-poverty expenditures has been disappointing. The distribution of 7.6 billion soles (about 40 percent of the total public budget in 1996) is mildly tilted towards the better-off in Peruvian society; i.e., the poorest obtain less of these expenditures than their population share. In large part this is due to the anti-poor distribution of higher education and hospital expenditures. Several specialized Government programs reach only a small proportion of the poor and direct public transfers play a significantly smaller role than private transfers do.

This report does not aim to provide detailed recommendations as to how poverty can be eradicated in Peru. While strategies to reduce poverty are necessary and important, they do carry the risk of oversimplifying a very complex and difficult task. In Peru, with about half of the population in poverty, poverty eradication will take a long time and require the coordinated efforts of all parts of society - the public, private, and voluntary sectors - and the international community.

The report does hold, however, that a much bigger impact could be achieved with available resources. First, economic and social policy making would need to be more closely integrated, informed by sound technical analyses and advice. Today, the many social policy programs operate independently; they try to reach their beneficiaries with different means and lack stringent evaluation. Second, and closely linked to the above, pro-poor policy formulation needs to be accompanied by thorough and good evaluation. This goes beyond the need for targeting and prioritization. It includes, for policymakers, the ability to assess whether certain interventions did indeed help or not. It also implies that policymakers and technicians are able to assess how *changes* in program nature and how *changes* in expenditures are distributed and what effect these changes have. Third, central coordination promises to be effective if it goes hand in hand with decentralized execution, involving other partners in the fight against poverty. Examples from other Latin American countries show that private-voluntary-public partnerships in poverty reduction at the local level can be extremely successful.

ACKNOWLEDGMENTS

This report is a product of the Peru Country Department, Latin America and the Caribbean Region of the World Bank. Jesko Hentschel led the team that prepared the report. The team included Alberto Chong (panel data analysis), Edgard Rodriguez (inequality analysis), and Vajeera Dorabawila (consumption definition, profile, and simulations). It also draws on background papers by Rafael Cortez (health and nutrition), Lucia Fort (indigenous people and gender) and Jaime Saavedra (labor market and education). Juan Diaz provided valuable support. The director of the Peru country department, Isabel Guerrero, and the lead economist, Ernesto May, provided overall guidance during the preparation of the report.

Thanks are due to many commentators and advisors in Peru, the World Bank and other international organizations, among them Javier Abugattas, Katherine Bain, Elena Conterno, Daniel Cotlear, Fritz DuBois, Willem van Eeghen, Javier Escobal, Adrian Fajardo, Rosa Flores, Pedro Francke, Carol Graham, Norman Hicks, Daniel Hinze, Fred Levy, Gilberto Moncada, Helena Ribe, Marcos Robles, Jose Antonio Rodriguez, Norbert Schady, Moises Ventocilla, Richard Webb, Kin Bing Wu, and Gabriel Ortiz de Zeballos. Many thanks also to Deborah Davis, who edited the report, and to Margarita Caro, who produced the final document.

We would like to acknowledge close cooperation, fruitful discussions, and the generous sharing of data information with both the Instituto Cuánto and the Peruvian Statistical Institute (Instituto Nacional de Estadistica e Información, INEI). Much of the material and statistics presented in this report are based on four different household surveys. Two of them are Living Standard Measurement Surveys (LSMS) by the independent Instituto Cuánto (*Encuesta Nacional de Hogares Sobre Niveles de Vida*, ENNIV 1994 and 1997); one is a national household survey by the National Statistical Institute INEI (*Encuesta Nacional de Hogares*, ENAHO 1996); and one is a survey on violence (*Encuesta de Hogares sobre Violencia*, ENHOVI 1997) by the same institute.

We welcome comments on the report. Please communicate such comments, or requests for the statistical programs used, to JHentschel@worldbank.org.

PERU - POBREZA Y DESARROLLO SOCIAL, 1994-1997

RESUMEN DEL INFORME

Este informe contiene la evaluación del progreso social en el Perú entre 1994 y 1997. En general, la evaluación presenta aspectos positivos pero también subraya varios elementos preocupantes. La buena noticia la constituye la mejora del bienestar social en los últimos años, la cual se verifica a través de distintos indicadores. La tasa de pobreza - el porcentaje de la población cuyo gasto total no cubre el costo de una canasta básica de consumo - disminuyó en varios puntos porcentuales y se encontró en 49 por ciento en 1997. Consecuentemente, casi 12 millones de peruanos eran considerados pobres. La pobreza extrema - aquellos hogares cuyo gasto no logra cubrir una canasta básica alimenticia -, por otro lado, también descendió de aproximadamente 19 a 15 por ciento. Sin embargo, quedaban tres y medio millones de peruanos en una grave situación de hambre y necesidad. La asistencia escolar se elevó ligeramente, la tasa de alfabetismo tuvo un ligero incremento de 87 a 90 por ciento y la población gozó de mejores niveles de salud en 1997. Lo más importante en este último aspecto es que disminuyó la tasa de desnutrición infantil en niños menores de cinco años. En 1997, aproximadamente 600,000 niños menores de cinco años-uno de cada cuatro- sufrían de desnutrición. El Cuadro 1 muestra la evolución de diversos indicadores de nivel de vida.

Cuadro 1: Indicadores Básicos[1]							
	Cambio[2]	Nacional		Urbana		Rural	
		1994	1997	1994	1997	1994	1997
Tasa de desnutrición (%)	√	30.0	23.8	17.4	12.2	44.7	37.3
Tasa de alfabetismo (%)	√	87.6	90.2	92.3	94.3	77.4	82.1
Tasa de pobreza (%)	√	53.5	49.0	46.1	40.4	67.0	64.7
Brecha de pobreza (%)	√	18.9	16.0	14.4	11.8	27.1	23.5
Tasa de pobreza extrema(%)	√	18.8	14.8	12.9	9.3	29.5	24.5
Desigualdad de ingresos, Gini	X	.469	.484	.437	.441	.494	.500
Trabajo de menores (%)	X	7.8	11.8	3.9	6.9	22.5	33.5
Matrícula escolar ('000)	√	4,880	5,080	2,960	3,030	1,920	2,050
Atención ambulatoria pública (4 semanas, miles)	√	1,760	2,990	1,250	2,160	510	830
Conex. servicios eléctricos (%)	√	68.8	73.7	93.7	97.4	23.2	30.3
Conex. servicios sanitarios (%)	√	48.2	58.6	73.4	84.3	2.4	11.6
Red pública de agua (%)	√	65.0	72.8	84.9	89.0	28.8	43.1
Viviendas con piso de tierra (%)	X	41.0	43.3	20.4	23.2	77.9	79.6

1   La definición de los indicadores se consigna al final de esta sección.
2   El símbolo '√' significa un cambio positivo, tal como la baja de la tasa de pobreza. El símbolo 'X' significa un cambio negativo.
Fuente: Estimados basados en ENNIV (1994, 1997)

Estas mejoras se deben, sin lugar a dudas, al favorable entorno económico general entre 1994 y 1997, con tasas reales de crecimiento per cápita de aproximadamente 3.5 por ciento. Este crecimiento, contrariamente a la creencia pública, sí generó empleo. La *Encuesta Nacional de Hogares Sobre Medición de Niveles de Vida* (ENNIV, Instituto Cuánto 1994 y 1997) permite estimar que se crearon cerca de 1.3 millones de puestos de trabajo adicionales en el mercado nacional, absorbiendo tanto el aumento poblacional como una tasa más alta de participación de la fuerza laboral. Sin embargo, muchos de estos nuevos puestos de trabajo fueron empleos informales, de modo que los trabajadores carecen de contratos de trabajo formales, seguro de pensiones o de salud. En el Perú, el emplo informal[1] es muy extenso, encontrándose desde hace tiempo en un nivel más o menos constante de aproximadamente 45 por ciento del empleo urbano, y siendo aún mayor en las zonas rurales. Las tendencias positivas del bienestar social, observadas en el Cuadro 1, se deben también a esfuerzos importantes del gobierno por mejorar las condiciones de vida. Entre 1994 y 1997, más de medio millón de familias se beneficiarón con conexiones de luz y agua; el sector de salud pública brindó atención a más de un millón adicional de pacientes ambulatorios por mes; y el número de niños que asisten a la escuela aumentó en 200,000.

Se debe mencionar, sin embargo, que existen aspectos preocupantes, muchos de ellos estan íntimamente ligados entre sí. El crecimiento económico y los programas gubernamentales no han llegado a todos por igual. En primer lugar, las desigualdades regionales han aumentado. Mientras algunas regiones muestran grandes avances, especialmente Lima, otras regiones muestran poco progreso, especialmente las zonas rurales andinas. El Cuadro 2 es una muestra del grado de diferencia por área geográfica que se da en los avances realizados entre 1994 y 1997. En la zona rural de la sierra, la pobreza general permanece estancada aún cuando el grado de severidad haya disminuido. Del total de la reducción de la pobreza, casi 80 por ciento proviene sólo de dos regiones: Lima y la región de sierra urbana. En comparaciones internacionales, Perú permanece entre aquellos países que tienen una variación extremadamente alta de nivel de ingreso regional.

Cuadro 2: Grado de Avances de Mejoras en Indicadores en Comparación al Promedio Nacional, 1994 – 1997			
	Pobreza	**Pobreza Extrema**	**Desnutrición**
Lima	√	√	√
Costa Urbana	X	√	X
Costa Rural	X	X	√
Sierra Urbana	√	√	√
Sierra Rural	X	X	X
Selva Urbana	X	√	√
Selva Rural	X	√	√
1 El símbolo '√' significa un desarrollo mejor que el promedio del país; el símbolo 'X' significa un desarollo peor que el promedio del país.			
<u>Fuente</u>: Estimados basados en ENNIV 1994-1997.			

---

[1]   La definición de informalidad utilizada en este estudio se consigna al final de esta sección.

En segundo lugar, el estudio encuentra también evidencia de que la desigualdad aumentó entre 1994 y 1997. Otros estudios[2] han señalado que durante las últimas décadas la desigualdad ha venido reduciéndose en el Perú hasta mediados de los noventa de manera sostenida, gracias al mayor acceso a activos claves como tierra y educación. En ese sentido, el pequeño aumento en la desigualdad que se registra entre 1994 y 1997, al considerar varios métodos de medición de la distribución del ingreso y la riqueza, implicaría una reversión de una tendencia positiva hacia una mayor equidad en el país. Por ello, este fenómeno debe ser observado muy de cerca por los encargados de diseñar las políticas sociales en el país. La inequidad tiene además efectos socio-económicos importantes. Los estudios recientes han demostrado que cuánto mayor es la desigualdad social, mayor es también la tendencia a la violencia. Asimismo, el progreso económico también se ve afectado, pues las sociedades mas desiguales ostentan bajos niveles de crecimiento.

El estudio encuentra dos factores detrás de estos aumentos en la desigualdad: en primer lugar, la mejora económica actual ha beneficiado mayormente a los peruanos con mejor nivel educativo frente a los que recibieron menos educación. Este es un patrón que la globalización y el cambio tecnológico reforzarán, por lo que resulta prioritario enfatizar la inversión en educación. En segundo lugar, el desarrollo regional ha variado notablemente. Esta diferencia en el desarrollo regional se refleja también en la distribución de las principales inversiones públicas: mientras que el gobierno se ha esforzado en llegar más a la población marginal de las zonas rurales, este esfuerzo se ha traducido sólo en forma parcial en beneficios perceptibles. Aproximadamente el 70 por ciento de los grandes logros en educación, salud e infraestructura se han dado en las ciudades (Cuadro 3).

Cuadro 3: Distribución del Nuevo Acceso a Servicios Básicos y Sociales, 1994-1997 *(Porcentaje)*			
	Urbano	**Rural**	**(Total)**
Agua	57	43	(100)
Electricidad	72	28	(100)
Saneamiento	78	22	(100)
Salud Ambulatoria	74	26	(100)
Educación, matrícula	33	67	(100)
<u>Fuente</u>: Estimados basados en ENNIV 1994, 1997			

En tercer lugar, entre 1994 y 1997 el desarrollo en el Perú fue inclusivo para muchos, pero exclusivo para otros. Existen aquí también aspectos positivos, como que las diferencias de género disminuyeron y que algunos grupos vulnerables como los conformados por los migrantes[3] o los que no poseen tierras, comparten los beneficios del desarrollo. No obstante, otros grupos aparentemente quedan a la zaga. En este segundo bloque el estudio identifica claramente a los pueblos indígenas[4], de los que su integración social y política todavía esta muy lejos de ser calnzada. Económicamente, los pueblos nativos han sufrido un retroceso importante: mientras que en 1994 una familia indígena tenía cuarenta por ciento más de posibilidades de ser pobre que una familia no indígena, en 1997 ese porcentaje se ha elevado a

---

[2]   Escobal, Javier, Máximo Torero y Jaime Saavedra. Los activos de los pobres. Cuadernos de Trabajo. Grupo de Análisis para el Desarrollo.Grade. Lima..Diciembre 1998.

[3]   La definición operativa de esta categoría se incluye al final de esta sección.

[4]   La definición operativa de esta categoría se incluye al final de esta sección.

casi cincuenta por ciento (Cuadro 4). El estudio identifica, al observar a estas mismas familias entre 1994 y 1997, que su situación no ha evolucionado tan favorablemente en relación al resto, aún teniendo en cuenta su bajo nivel de educación, el reducido acceso a los servicios y a la propiedad de tierras o viviendas. Lograr el progreso de los indígenas pobres es un reto más complejo que el de los pobres urbanos, cuya integración a los mercados es más sencilla de lograr, lo que implica la necesidad de un esfuerzo especial.

Cuadro 4: ¿Mayor o Menor Probabilidad de ser Pobre? Proporciones Relativas de Pobreza entre Grupos (por ciento)	Nacional	
	1994	1997
Indígenas (vernáculo hablantes)	+40.2	+48.7
Infantes (0-5 años)	+26.0	+27.0
niños (6-14 años)	+24.5	+25.5
jóvenes, (15-17 años)	+ 5.5	+ 8.6
Familias rurales sin tierras	+ 3.4	-4.0
Familias rurales dirigidas por viudos	-5.0	-14.2
Familias dirigidas por mujeres	-12.8	-16.5
Migrantes	-16.0	-18.0
Fuente: Estimados basados en ENNIV. El Cuadro registra el riesgo relativo de ser pobre, es decir, el riesgo absoluto de ser pobre en comparación con otros grupos. El signo positivo significa que este grupo tiene mayor proporción de pobres que el resto de la población; el símbolo negativo indica lo contrario.		

La situación social de la niñez continúa siendo difícil. Dada la mayor fecundidad de las familias pobres, la problemática de la pobreza está estrechamente vinculada a la población infantil. Las tasas de pobreza que prevalecen entre los más jóvenes de la sociedad peruana continúan dentro de un rango mayor a cualquier otro grupo de edad. Y aún cuando las tasas de pobreza hayan disminuido, la reducción es leve y mucho menor de lo que fue para otros grupos. Los datos de la encuesta muestran también el problema del trabajo de menores por cuanto cada vez es mayor el número de menores cuyas edades fluctúan entre 6 y 14 años que deben trabajar para contribuir al sostenimiento familiar. Entre 1994 y 1997 ha aumentado el número de menores de edad que trabajan más de 15 horas semanales en 241 mil. Diversos estudios han señalado el impacto negativo que el trabajo de menores puede tener sobre la educación, comprometiendo el futuro de estos niños. En el caso de los jóvenes que ya están en edad de trabajar, el estudio señala que el desempleo juvenil tiene cifras muy altas: 18 por ciento para las mujeres y 14 por ciento para los hombres en Lima (1996), con una tendencia creciente.

QUÉ ES LO QUE AYUDA AL PROGRESO DE UN HOGAR?

La finalidad del informe no es describir la situación de los pobres dentro de la sociedad peruana ni bosquejar un "perfil de pobreza" sobre la base de la última información disponible. Existen ya muchos estudios sobre ello. Más bien, el estudio busca evaluar aquellos factores que determinan que las familias progresen o queden rezagadas en el tiempo, mediante la comparación de los resultados de las encuestas de 1994 y 1997. Esta evaluación es de especial importancia para los responsables de diseñar las políticas pertinentes. Por ejemplo, una visión estática podría revelar que el empleo informal tiene fuerte correlación con la pobreza. En cambio, una visión dinámica puede ir más allá, al responder si las familias vinculadas predominantemente al mercado informal tienen mayor o menor probabilidad relativa de salir de la pobreza.

A través del tiempo han habido varios factores que han influido tanto en forma positiva como negativa en el bienestar de los hogares. Los resultados más destacables son los siguientes:

♦ Los hogares cuyos ingresos provenían del sector informal han progresado más que los del sector formal. Esto es cierto tanto en zonas urbanas como en el caso del empleo informal fuera del campo en zonas rurales.

♦ Los hogares más numerosos no han progresado al mismo grado de aquéllos menos numerosos.

♦ Una mayor educación implica un progreso más rápido.

♦ El acceso a servicios como al crédito e infraestructura básica no solamente representa una ayuda inmediata, sino que ayuda a progresar más rápidamente en formas no conectadas directamente con dicho acceso. El estudio encuentra evidencia muy clara respecto de la importancia que representa el acceso a varios servicios: brindar servicios en forma conjunta genera sinergias.

El informe también incluye algunos resultados respecto a la incidencia e impacto que tiene la violencia sobre las familias pobres urbanas. La violencia es una de las preocupaciones principales de los pobres urbanos. Las tasas de incidencia de varios tipos de violencia difieren de acuerdo al grupo de pobreza, estando los pobres doblemente expuestos a la agresión física que aquellos cuya posición es mejor dentro de la sociedad. Consecuentemente, su sentido de inseguridad es mayor.

PERSPECTIVAS PARA LA REDUCCIÓN DE LA POBREZA – CRECIMIENTO Y EMPLEO

Una de las mayores preocupaciones dentro del debate público en el Perú es establecer si el crecimiento ha creado empleos y si esto ha servido para reducir la pobreza. La respuesta es afirmativa. El crecimiento en los años pasados ciertamente ha creado empleos: aproximadamente 1.3 millones más de personas han tenido empleo remunerado en 1997 que en 1994. La mayor parte de los puestos de trabajo tuvieron su origen en el sector informal, pero ello no implica que estuvieran mal remunerados. La tendencia que preocupa es que la productividad en la zona urbana no parece aumentar y, consecuentemente, los salarios reales en el mejor de los casos se mantienen constantes.

En principio, el patrón de crecimiento en el Perú debiera haber favorecido a los pobres, porque los sectores donde los trabajadores y sus dependientes tienden mayormente a ser pobres (construcción, comercio y agricultura) han sido los que crecieron más rápidamente. Aparentemente esto ha servido para ayudar a los pobres en el ramo de construcción y comercio, pero no tanto en el sector agrícola, donde la reducción de la pobreza ha sido menos rápida de lo que se esperaba. El crecimiento en el agro no ha generado mayor impacto en cuanto a empleo. Esto posiblemente se haya debido a que dicho crecimiento apenas haya revertido el "retroceso en la productividad" que se dio como resultado de la recesión existente en la agricultura a comienzos de la década. Ello implica que el posterior crecimiento de la agricultura ha conducido a recuperar niveles de trabajo más intenso, es decir horarios más largos por trabajador, pero no más empleo.

Varias simulaciones demuestran la importancia del crecimiento en relación con la reducción de la pobreza en el Perú. Si bien las simulaciones son sencillas, permiten mostrar que el tipo de crecimiento y su distribución regional es importante para el impacto sobre la pobreza. Si el crecimiento está basado mayormente en la agricultura, construcción y comercio, y su impacto se refleja mayormente en las zonas rurales, la reducción de la pobreza será mayor en el corto plazo. Es por ello que debe cuidarse que las políticas no sean discriminatorias en contra de dichos sectores.

El Gasto Social y la Lucha contra la Pobreza

Es importante analizar la distribución del gasto social y su papel en la lucha contra la pobreza. Al examinar la incidencia de unos 7.6 mil millones de soles destinados por el gobierno en 1996 para estos fines (cerca de 40 por ciento del total del presupuesto del gasto público), se puede ver que éste está ligeramente orientado hacia las personas de mejor situación dentro de la sociedad peruana. Ello quiere decir que los más pobres obtienen menos de estos gastos que la distribución que les correspondería en relación a su peso en la población (Cuadro 5). Esto se debe en gran parte a que los gastos en educación superior y atención hospitalaria están sesgados en contra de los pobres, entre otros.

Cuadro 5: Distribución Agregada de Gastos Sociales, 1996	
Quintil	Proporción del gasto total
1 (los más pobres)	16.6
2	18.6
3	21.2
4	22.4
5 (los más ricos)	21.1
(Incluye educación, salud, programas de lucha contra la pobreza y vivienda)	
Fuente: Estimados basados en ENAHO 1996 y Presupuesto Público 1996.	

Varios de los programas gubernamentales especializados llegan a muy pocos de los pobres y las transferencias directas de fondos públicos tienen un papel notablemente menor al de las transferencias del sector privado, incluyendo en éstas las transferencias en dinero o especies de familiares, amigos, organizaciones religiosas, voluntarias, etc. El programa de alimentos PRONAA y el fondo social FONCODES son los programas que tienen mayor cobertura y menores tasas de escape (mejor focalización), pero los programas de crédito para vivienda, así como los de infraestructura de COOPOP, FONAVI e INFES llegaron solamente a unos cuantos de los pobres en 1996. La ayuda alimentaria tiene el mayor efecto positivo en las zonas rurales del Perú. Sin embargo, en el país las transferencias de fondos privados tienen, por lo general un papel significativamente más importante que las transferencias de fondos del sector público.

DE LAS ESTRATEGIAS SECTORIALES A UN ENFOQUE AMPLIO Y CONSISTENTE PARA COMBATIR LA POBREZA

El informe no pretende ofrecer recomendaciones detalladas sobre la forma cómo se puede erradicar la pobreza en el Perú. Su objetivo es proporcionar una rápida retroalimentación sobre los desarrollos sociales y la pobreza, según la última *Encuesta Nacional de Hogares Sobre Medición de Niveles de Vida* publicada por Instituto Cuánto en Junio de 1998, combinando dicha información con un análisis de políticas pertinentes sobre patrones de crecimiento y la distribución de los gastos sociales. Cabe señalar que si bien las estrategias globales para reducir la pobreza son necesarias, no constituyen un remedio inmediato para un problema tan complejo de superar como el de la pobreza. En el Perú, donde casi la mitad de su población está constituida por pobres, la erradicación de la pobreza tomará mucho tiempo y se requiere del esfuerzo coordinado de toda la sociedad –el sector público, el sector privado y las organizaciones voluntarias–, al igual que el de la comunidad internacional.

El informe tampoco recomienda la creación de nuevos programas o modificaciones a los programas actuales. En líneas generales, los programas de lucha contra la pobreza en el Perú ponen énfasis en los sectores correctos, al incluir ayuda de emergencia con enfoque nutricional y infraestructura básica. Sin embargo, el estudio revela que podría lograrse un impacto mucho mayor con los fondos disponibles:

Primeramente, el diseño de las políticas sociales y económicas necesitarían estar mejor integrados, así como basados en mayor nivel de análisis y asesoría. Actualmente, un gran número de programas de política social opera en forma independiente, tratando de llegar a los beneficiarios a través de diferentes medios y carece de una evaluación estricta. Solamente en el Ministerio de la Presidencia existen seis programas en el sector educación –independientes y adicionales a los del Ministerio de Educación-. Los programas de nutrición son muchos y los administran los Ministerios de Finanzas (Vaso de Leche), de Promoción de la Mujer y Desarrollo Humano (PRONAA), de Salud (Programa de Salud Básica, PACFO) de Educación y de la Presidencia (FONCODES). Los gastos de muchos de estos programas, aunque ciertamente bien intencionados, no llegan a los más pobres de la sociedad y a menudo están aislados entre sí. Actualmente se utiliza diversos mecanismos para focalizar las acciones de los programas públicos, sin que exista concordancia entre ellos. Todo lo anterior señala que se podría lograr una mayor reducción de la pobreza si las intervenciones fuesen integradas, es decir si se brindan en forma conjunta y coordinada. En Perú, existen actualmente decretos antagónicos que dan poder tanto al Ministerio de la Presidencia como al Consejo de Coordinación Social CIAS en este campo, aunque ninguna de las instituciones tiene verdadero poder. Si bien el CIAS ha reiniciado recientemente sus esfuerzos, se requiere un potenciamiento de las acciones de coordinación, tal vez mediante la integración de los ministerios sociales en un consejo mucho más poderoso para la elaboración de políticas en este campo.

En segundo lugar, e íntimamente ligado a lo anterior, la formulación de políticas en favor de los pobres requiere mejores y más completos sistemas de evaluación. Esto va más allá de la necesidad de fijar objetivos y prioridades. Los diseñadores de las políticas deben poder evaluar si determinadas intervenciones fueron o no de utilidad. Ello implica que se pueda evaluar la forma cómo se lleva a cabo la distribución y cúal es el efecto de los cambios, tanto en la naturaleza de los programas como en los gastos.

En tercer lugar, la coordinación central promete ser efectiva si va de la mano con la ejecución descentralizada, involucrando a otros socios en la lucha contra la pobreza. Los ejemplos que brindan otros países de América Latina muestran cómo la asociación entre organismos privados-voluntarios y públicos puede tener mucho éxito en la reducción de la pobreza a nivel local. Una de las razones para el éxito de estas asociaciones es que cada una de las organizaciones contribuye con su propia ventaja comparativa. El gobierno central pone el apoyo financiero y la organización, el gobierno municipal el conocimiento del ámbito local, y las organizaciones voluntarias o no gubernamentales y organizaciones de base contribuyen a menudo con una comprensión amplia y directa de los problemas de los pobres.

Definiciones

Atención ambulatoria pública:

Número de atenciones ambulatorias (en miles) por (4 semanas, miles) la red de salud pública en un período de cuatro semanas.

Brecha de pobreza (%):

Diferencia entre el gasto promedio de los pobres y la línea de pobreza, expresada como porcentaje de la línea de pobreza.

Coeficiente de Gini:

Indicador utilizado para representar el grado de desigualdad en la distribución del ingreso.

Conexión de servicios eléctricos (%):

Porcentaje de la población con conexión a sistema público de electricidad.

Conexión de servicios sanitarios (%):

Porcentaje de la población con conexión a sistema público de desagüe.

Desigualdad de ingresos, Gini:

La variable ingreso considera los ingresos provenientes del autoempleo, salarios, transferencias y rentas de propiedades.

ENAHO:

Encuesta Nacional de Hogares realizada por el Instituto Nacional de Estadística e Informática (INEI). Ha sido realizada semestralmente desde 1995.

ENNIV:

Encuesta Nacional de Hogares sobre Medición de Niveles de Vida, realizada por el Instituto Cuánto dirigida a medir la situación social y económica de las personas. Ha sido realizada en 1991, 1994 y 1997.

Informalidad:

Referida a las actividades de empleo y autoempleo no sujetas al pago de impuestos, seguro (IPSS), sin firma de contratos, sin derechos a vacaciones ni sindicatos.

Indígenas: Para efectos del presente informe se entiende como familia indígena a toda aquella familia cuya jefe dice que su lengua materna sea el quechua, aymara, campa u otra lengua nativa. Esta variable "lengua nativa" ha sido utilizada como proxy de etnicidad, dado que aparte de la lengua se entiende que las familias indígenas comparten además tradiciones, vestimenta, creencias, etc.

Matrícula escolar ('000):   Número total de matriculados en primaria y secundaria.

Migrantes: Hogares cuyo jefe mencionó que no haber nacido en la localidad (pueblo, localidad de residencia actual).

Red pública de agua (%):   Porcentaje de la población con conexión a sistema público de agua.

Tasa de alfabetismo (%):   Porcentaje de la población por encima de los 6 años de edad que sabe leer y escribir.

Tasa de desnutrición (%):   Porcentaje de niños menores de cinco años con una desviación estándar de talla mayor a dos, por debajo de la norma internacional ajustada correspondiente a su edad.

Tasa de pobreza (%) :   Porcentaje de la población incapaz de cubrir el costo de una canasta básica de consumo. Al valor de esta canasta de consumo también se le denomina línea de pobreza.

Tasa de pobreza extrema (%)   Porcentaje de la población cuyo gasto no logra cubrir una canasta muy austera.

Trabajo de menores (%):   Porcentaje de todos los niños, de 6 a 14 años de edad, que trabajan más de 15 horas semanales.

Viviendas con piso de tierra (%):   Porcentaje de la población que reside en viviendas con piso de tierra.

1. OVERVIEW

POVERTY AND SOCIAL DEVELOPMENTS, 1994-1997

This report evaluates social progress in Peru from 1994 to 1997. It carries mainly good news but also reports several worrisome developments. The good news is that social welfare improved over the three years - and this is true when looked at from a variety of angles. The poverty rate, the percentage of the population not able to finance a basic basket of goods, has declined by several percentage points and now stands at 49 percent - roughly 12 million Peruvians are therefore considered poor. Severe consumption poverty - an extremely austere measure - has also declined, from about 19 to 15 percent. This does, nevertheless, leave three and a half million Peruvians in the immediate danger of hunger and deprivation. In line with consumption poverty rates, school attendance has risen slightly, literacy rates increased from 87 to 90 percent, and the population is healthier. Most important among the latter, the rate of malnutrition for children below the age of five has further declined. About 600,000 children younger than five, or one in every four, were malnourished in 1997.

These improvements are without doubt due to the favorable overall economic environment, with per capita real growth rates from 1994 to 1997 at about 3.5 percent. This growth, contrary to public belief, did create jobs. We estimate that about 1.3 million additional jobs were created in the economy, absorbing both a population increase and a higher participation rate in the labor force. Many of these new jobs are informal jobs, however, so workers are without formal contracts, pension insurance, or health insurance. Informality in Peru remains at a constant rate of about 45 percent of urban employment, even higher in rural areas. The positive social welfare trends are also due to substantial Government efforts: from 1994 to 1997, more than half a million households received water, electricity, and sanitation connections; the public health sector attended more than one million additional ambulatory patients per month; and 200,000 more children were in school in 1997 compared to 1994.

But there are also some worrisome developments to report - and most of them are closely knit together. Economic growth and Government programs have not been spread equally and have not benefited everybody. First, regional disparities have grown, with some regions showing enormous progress, especially Lima, and other regions falling relatively behind, especially the rural areas in the highlands. In the rural Sierra, overall poverty remains stagnant while its severity has declined. Of the total reduction in poverty, almost 80 percent stemmed from two regions alone: Lima and the urban Sierra. In international comparisons Peru remains one of the countries with an extremely high variation of regional income.

Second, with regional disparities increasing we also find some evidence that inequality has risen in the three years under study - a small increase in inequality can be observed when using several measurement methods and when looking at the distribution of income or wealth alike. This increase in inequality comes after a decrease over a long time period – from 1985 to 1994. And although it is not at all certain that inequality will continue to rise, policymakers should closely watch it. Evidence now exists that more unequal societies tend to be more violent societies. Economic progress also depends on equality, with more unequal societies showing a worse growth record. And, clearly, inequality and poverty are also directly linked:

for any given national income, the more unequal the society, the higher the poverty rate. We find two factors behind these inequality increases in Peru. The more educated Peruvians profited more from the current upswing than the less educated. Obviously, this means that improving the quality of primary and secondary education would decrease inequality. Additionally, regional development varied strongly and contributed to the small rise in inequality. This different regional development is also mirrored in the distribution of major public investments: While the government has made an effort to reach out more to the marginal rural population, this effort has only partially translated into measurable benefits. Of the large achievements in education, health and infrastructure, about 70 percent have been in cities.

Third, Peru's development in the past years has been inclusive for many but exclusive for others. While we find gender differences narrowing and vulnerable groups such as migrants and the landless sharing the benefits of development, certain groups appear to have fallen further behind or remain highly at risk of deprivation. One group is clearly the indigenous population. Their social and political integration is still far from achieved. And we now find that even economically the native population has fallen further behind: while in 1994 an indigenous family was 40 percent more likely to be poor than a non-native family, in 1997 they were almost 50 percent more likely to be poor. Additionally, observing hundreds of the same families from 1994 to 1997, the indigenous families have clearly done worse, even if we control for their lower educational training, lower access to services, and lower land or housing ownership compared to the non-native population.

The social situation of children remains bleak. The youngest in Peruvian society continue to have far higher poverty and severe poverty rates than any other age group. And although poverty rates decreased, the drop was slight and much less than for other groups. Also, the survey data tells a sad story about child labor as more and more youngsters between the ages of 6 and 14 work. In addition to children, many young adolescents are not faring well in Peruvian society. Youth unemployment is very high, 18 percent for females and 14 percent for males in Lima in 1996, and shows a rising trend. In international comparison, while Peru reduced infant mortality from 54 (1990) to 42 deaths per 1,000 live births in 1996, it is still lagging behind the regional achievements for countries of its income level and it places Peru among the worst in the Latin American region.

This report does not aim to describe the situation of the poor in Peruvian society - to sketch a "poverty profile". Many other studies have done this. Rather, we are interested in assessing what determines whether families get ahead or fall behind over time. This is of special relevance to policymakers. For example, a static view might tell us that informal employment is a strong correlate of poverty. But a view over time will show whether the depth of poverty increases if a household is linked predominantly to the informal market.

WHAT HELPS HOUSEHOLDS ADVANCE?

A number of factors have influenced household welfare over time, in both positive and negative ways. First, surprisingly, households were more likely to advance if their income stemmed from the informal sector than from the formal sector. This is true in urban areas as well as in informal off-farm employment in rural areas. Second, household size matters.

Larger families have done worse than smaller ones – this relationship can work through higher dependency ratios that can limit the ability of households to save. Third, more education means faster advancement. Finally, savings and access to basic services like water, electricity or sanitation is not only of immediate support to households but helps them advance faster in ways not just directly connected to services access. We also find that bundling of such services matters: providing two services jointly has a more positive effect than the sum of providing each one separately.

The report also includes some findings about the incidence and impact of urban violence on the families of the poor. While we cannot link insecurity directly to welfare developments, violence is one of the main preoccupations of the urban poor. The incidence of various types of violence differs by poverty group, the poor being about twice as likely to be exposed to physical aggression as the better-off in society. Consequently, their feeling of insecurity is higher.

PROSPECTS FOR POVERTY REDUCTION - GROWTH AND EMPLOYMENT LINKS

One of the biggest concerns in the Peruvian public debate on poverty is whether growth has created employment and whether this has led to poverty reduction. We find that growth has indeed created employment; about 1.3 million more people have been in remunerated employment in 1997 compared to 1994. The majority of jobs were created in the informal sector but they were not necessarily low-paying jobs. A worrisome trend is that urban productivity does not seem to be rising and, consequently, real wages are flat at best.

On face value, Peru's growth path over the past years was pro-poor because the sectors where workers and their dependents are most likely to be poor (construction, commerce and agriculture) grew fastest. This appears to have helped the poor in construction and commerce. In agriculture, however, poverty reduction was slower than could have been hoped for. Employment creation as a corollary to agricultural growth was not strong. This could be due to a productivity backlog stemming from the recession at the beginning of the 1990s, implying that agricultural growth first led to more intensive work, i.e. longer hours per employed person.

A number of simulations show how important growth remains for poverty reduction in Peru. The simulations are very simple and, for example, do not take into account that workers will move between areas and sectors or that the employment effect of growth will differ between sectors. The simulations do show, however, that the type of growth and its regional distribution will matter - the more growth is based in agriculture, construction and commerce, and the more its impacts filter through to the rural highlands and lowlands, the more poverty will be reduced in the short run. While the growth pattern should not be artificially tilted towards such sectors, investment in these sectors will depend on a continuation of non-discrimination policies.

SOCIAL EXPENDITURE

The distribution of social and anti-poverty expenditures has been disappointing. The distribution of 7.6 billion soles (about 40 percent of the total public budget in 1996) is mildly tilted towards the better-off in Peruvian society; i.e., the poorest obtain less of these expenditures than their population share. In large part this is due to the anti-poor distribution of higher education and hospital expenditures.

Several specialized Government programs reach only a small proportion of the poor and direct public transfers play a significantly smaller role than private transfers do. The nutrition program PRONAA and the social fund FONCODES have the highest coverage and lowest leakage rates but the housing credit programs as well as the infrastructure programs of COOPOP, FONAVI and INFES reached only few of the poor. Food aid has the largest positive effect in rural Peru, where the severe poverty rate would have been 3 percent higher had these programs not existed in 1997. However, private transfers generally play a significantly more important role than public transfers in the rural and urban areas alike.

FROM INDIVIDUAL SECTOR STRATEGIES TO A CONSISTENT AND BROAD-BASED ANTI-POVERTY FOCUS

The report does not aim to provide detailed recommendations as to how poverty can be eradicated in Peru. Rather, it presents a quick feedback about social developments and poverty based on the new Living Standard Measurement data from the Instituto Cuánto released in June 1998, and on policy-relevant analysis of growth patterns and the distribution of social expenditures. While strategies to reduce poverty are necessary and important, they do carry the risk of oversimplifying a very complex and difficult task. In Peru, with about half of the population in poverty, poverty eradication will take a long time and require the coordinated efforts of all parts of society - the public, private, and voluntary sectors - and the international community.

The report also does not recommend the creation of new programs, nor does it make a statement about the appropriate size and mix of programs. In broad lines, we find that the Peruvian anti-poverty programs with their mix of emergency help, nutritional focus, and infrastructure emphasize the right areas. However, we believe that a much bigger impact could be achieved with available funds.

First, economic and social policy making would need to be more closely integrated, informed by sound technical analyses and advice. Today, the many social policy programs operate independently; they try to reach their beneficiaries with different means and lack stringent evaluation. The Ministry of the Presidency alone has six programs in the education sector – outside and in addition to those of the Ministry of Education. Nutrition programs are plenty and administered by the ministries of Finance (Vaso de Leche), Women and Human Development (PRONAA), Health (Basic Health Program, PACFO), and Education as well as the Ministry of the Presidency (FONCODES). Expenditures of many of these programs, although well intended, do not reach the poorest in society and are often isolated in nature. Many different poverty maps and targeting mechanisms are currently employed, and these need to be harmonized. We find that poverty is reduced most effectively when if interventions

4

are integrated, that is provided jointly and in a coordinated way. In Peru, conflicting decrees empowering the Ministry of the Presidency and the Social Coordination Council (CIAS) currently exist – but neither institution has true power or manpower. Without integrating social ministries into the much more powerful council for economic policy making, weak coordination of social programs is likely to continue.

Second, and closely linked to the above, pro-poor policy formulation needs to be accompanied by thorough and good evaluation. This goes beyond the need for targeting and prioritization. It includes, for policymakers, the ability to assess whether certain interventions did indeed help or not. It also implies that policymakers and technicians are able to assess how *changes* in program nature and how *changes* in expenditures are distributed and what effect these changes have.

Third, central coordination promises to be effective if it goes hand in hand with decentralized execution, involving other partners in the fight against poverty. Examples from other Latin American countries show that private-voluntary-public partnerships in poverty reduction at the local level can be extremely successful. One reason is that each organization brings its comparative advantage to the table: central government brings finance and organization; municipal government brings local knowledge; and non-governmental organizations (NGOs) often bring a good and direct understanding of the problems of the poor. For this latter point the report has some evidence: In 1996, NGO-administered programs had a significantly better targeting record than most public programs and matched the good targeting results of FONCODES and PRONAA.

OUTLINE

This report is structured as follows. Section 2 contains a precautionary warning. It is a short recap of what household surveys can and cannot do, including an assessment of the reliability of poverty statistics. Section 3 looks at national and regional indicators of well-being between 1994 and 1997, and at why inequality rose between the two years. Section 4 presents our findings as to which groups in society did and did not benefit from the general rise in living standards in Peru. Further, we examine which main factors are responsible for such welfare changes. Section 5 examines the prospects for poverty reduction, given various growth rates of the economy, different assumptions about inequality and - most importantly - different types of growth patterns. Section 6 takes a look at the distribution of social expenditures in 1996, i.e., which groups were and were not reached by the Government's large social programs. Section 7 describes key institutional ingredients for developing successful poverty reduction strategies. The Annexes of this document give detailed information on data sources and definitions, methodologies, and report on a number of robustness tests of the results.

2. POVERTY RATES AS POLICY GOALS?

Much of the current political debate in Peru concerns whether poverty rates have fallen or risen over recent years. The prominence of poverty rates in the public debate is partly due to the Government having set clear goals of poverty reduction. It is also partly due to a heated public debate about social conditions in Peru. Before launching into poverty measurement, profiles, and correlates in the next section, we briefly want to argue in this section that, yes, setting poverty reduction goals is important and laudable. However, estimates of poverty rates are much more fragile than often thought. Furthermore, lifting people out of poverty has a much broader meaning than raising them above a poverty line.

Poverty rate estimates are based on household surveys, which are important and indispensable tools for poverty analyses and hence crucial for policy formulation. For example, the geographical distribution of poverty and severe poverty is a very important tool for expenditure targeting. Household surveys are indispensable for analyzing the distribution and coverage of public programs - which groups in society obtain what from the public purse. Similarly, they can serve to track enrollment rates, illness patterns, service access, and literacy rates at relatively moderate cost based on population samples and are therefore much less costly than population censuses. Surveys also help to determine the causes of poverty and well-being, as well as the factors influencing malnutrition and child mortality rates. Studies covering these and many other topics have been used in policy making in Peru for many years.

But poverty analysis based on such surveys is, by its very nature, not an exact science. The choice of poverty lines and the determination of consumption and income depend on a vast amount of assumptions which, if changed only slightly, can produce quite different poverty rates. It is, therefore, not surprising that different surveys will produce different poverty rates, as is the case in Peru right now. The Statistical Institute INEI and Instituto Cuánto have, for example, quite different questionnaires trying to capture household food expenditures. With different questions for different types of products or product categories, it is only logical that estimates of consumption and poverty will differ. This does not mean that one is more accurate than the other is. Whether poverty is 45, 49, or 53 percent should, in the end, not be at the center of attention. However, whether and to what degree poverty increased or decreased, using a consistent and common methodology is of importance to policymakers. Some of these aspects are further explored in Annex 2.

The fact that poverty calculations are based on a *sample* of households, hence a subset of the Peruvian population, also carries implications. Samples are designed to reproduce the whole population but they can never be as exact as information that covers everybody in the country. Hence, they carry a margin of error, as do poverty rates calculated from these sample surveys. Graph 1 shows what this margin of error means in the case of Peru. We use the

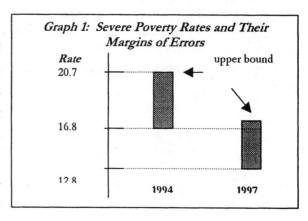

Graph 1: Severe Poverty Rates and Their Margins of Errors

calculated severe poverty rate as an example.[5] The two columns indicate the range in which we are very confident that the true severe poverty rate lies.[6] As can be seen, while we estimate that severe poverty has dropped substantially from 18.8 to 14.8 percent between 1994 and 1997, drawing such confidence intervals around them is quite revealing. If, indeed, we were at the lower end of the interval in 1994 and at the upper end in 1997, the rates for the two years might actually be very similar. And, on the contrary, if the true 1994 rate was 20 percent in 1994 and the true value for 1998 was at the lower end, around 13 percent, the drop in severe poverty can actually be bigger than we estimate here.

Further, while a policy focus on lifting people over the poverty line is laudable, poverty has obviously a much broader meaning. Income or consumption are only *means* of attaining better lives, and not *ends* in themselves. Lower malnutrition in children, better health of the population, longer lives, lower maternal and infant mortality rates, higher literacy, less hunger, more safety, less discrimination in work and social life, and more active participation in political and social affairs of communities and the country characterize better and less poor societies. And several of these other dimensions might not be linked to only consumption poverty: crime and violence might effect large parts of the population, discrimination in the job market can exist against certain groups in society, or children might be malnourished although they grow up in rather affluent households.

In conclusion, the answer to the question whether poverty rates should be policy goals is clearly *yes*. This commits policy to serving the most marginalized groups in society. However, policy makers need to be aware of the often quite fragile nature of such poverty estimates. And finally, reducing poverty rates is only a means to helping people live healthier, longer and better lives.

---

[5]   The severe poverty rate presented here is not strictly comparable with the extreme poverty rate generally reported due to the specifics of our consumption definition. See Annex 2 of this report.

[6]   The ranges indicate that we can be 95 percent confident that the true severe poverty rates lie within the upper and lower bounds of the interval.

3. POVERTY, INEQUALITY, AND SOCIAL DEVELOPMENTS, 1994-1997

This section provides basic statistics on poverty and social development in Peru since 1994. It takes a close regional look at where this progress has been faster and where slower and also assesses who in society has profited most from public investments in five areas: water, sanitation, electricity, education, and health. Finally, we explore the recent increase in inequality and trace it to its underlying causes.

BASIC DEVELOPMENTS

Indicators Used. We aim to look at social progress in Peru from a number of different angles. First, we use outcome indicators of the development of society - the rate of children below the age of five being malnourished and the literacy rate of the population.[7] Second are poverty indicators. Throughout this report, poverty is defined as a state in which the affected population has per capita expenditures less than needed to purchase a very basic basket of food and non-food goods. *Whenever we talk about poverty in this report we employ consumption per capita as the welfare measure.* The derivation of the cost of the basic basket of goods (which then comprises the poverty line) is somewhat different than generally applied in Peru. Especially, for comparison reasons between the two household survey years, 1994 and 1997, we had to make a number of important but tedious adjustments, as explained in detail in Annex 2 of this report.[8] More important than the percentage of the population below this imaginary line is *how far* the poor are away from it. For this we use the poverty gap to measure the resources necessary to bring all individuals to the poverty line. This is expressed as a proportion of the poverty line itself. We also use an additional, much more austere poverty line, to find those in the Peruvian population at risk of acute hunger and deprivation. Third, we compute inequality measures for consumption, wealth and income. The common indicator used here is the Gini coefficient, a measure that varies between 0 (totally equal society) to 1 (completely unequal society). Fourth, we record rates of child labor, defined as children age 6 to 14 year working more than 15 per hours per week. Starting from the position that child labor, especially at such young ages, is detrimental to both health and learning possibilities, we hope to find low and declining values.

---

[7] Both rates are derived from the LSMS (ENNIV 1994 and 1997) carried out by the Instituto Cuánto. The malnutrition calculations are for stunting (height for age), defining a child as malnourished if it is more than two standard deviations below the age-adjusted international norm. This is in line with other studies of malnutrition in Peru. One of the crucial assumptions in these studies is that age-specific norms of height and weight are homogenous in the country, i.e. that they do not vary by location or ethnic group.

[8] Some of these adjustments change the consumption aggregate supplied by Instituto Cuánto for both survey years. As explained in Annex 2, our major deviations from Cuánto's methodology include: (a) leaving the total bundle of goods entering into the calculation of the poverty line constant (while in Peru generally only the food basket is left unchanged), (b) excluding rent from the consumption aggregate as the survey question in this section changed significantly from 1994 and 1997, (c) interpreting the benefit transfer from social programs differently, and (d) using a different regional price deflation method.

Fifth, we are interested in total school enrollments and the number of ambulatory care visits to the total public health network. Obviously, these are only inputs, as by these sheer numbers we cannot tell the quality of education or *why* more people sought care in public health facilities - access and/or quality might have improved or people might also be more in need of care because their health deteriorated. Finally, we record the percentage of the population with access to sanitation, water, and electricity and the percentage of the population living in homes with mud floors.

While we will look below at the dispersion of some of these indicators by groups of people or by region, there are aspects of social development that we do not assess here. We do not look at, for example, whether different groups have secure property rights and the possibility of enforcing these rights; i.e., whether they have equal and fair access to the justice system. Similarly, social progress of society will also be a function of the degree to which families and communities participate in local and regional decision-making and of how society integrates differences in cultural values and beliefs.

Developments 1994 to 1997. Looked at from different angles, Peru has made progress in many areas during the three years. Table 1 contains the six different types of indicators outlined above. Malnutrition rates (for stunting) decreased substantially, in both urban and rural areas. We estimate that about one out of four children below the age of five is now malnourished, down from almost one in three in 1994. However, this leaves more than 600,000 children malnourished, which will lower their learning ability and make them much more vulnerable to illness - now and later in their lives as well. The literacy rate of the Peruvian population above six years of age increased and now reaches 90 percent.

Poverty decreased in the past several years and this is a robust result, quite independent of the poverty line chosen.[9] An especially positive development was the reduction of the severe poverty rate, from almost 19 to about 15 percent. If these are the true numbers (given the margin of error described in the last section), this means that 600,000 Peruvians have managed to find livelihoods that helped them out of extreme consumption deprivation. However, 3.5 million people remain in such immediate danger. The proportion of the population in poverty, not able to finance a basic basket of food and non-food goods, decreased as well but remains very high. Half of the population, or 12 million people, were poor in 1997. And as we have seen when looking at severe poverty rates, the reduction in poverty is not only limited to the part of the population having consumption expenditures near the poverty line. If this were the case, the poverty gap indicator (a measure of the depth of poverty in relation to the poverty line) would not show significant declines. As can be observed in the table, though, the gap has been reduced quite substantially, especially in rural areas.

Notwithstanding the decline in poverty, however, important inequality measures show a (modest) rise. Although Table 1 reports that the distribution of consumption, especially in rural Peru, is less skewed in 1997 than in 1994, the distribution of both income and wealth – which include savings and hence the accumulation of wealth - appears to have become more unequal in recent years.

---

[9] We varied the poverty line over a wide range and found that poverty rates decreased quite homogeneously.

		National		Urban		Rural	
	Table 1: Basic Indicators *(percent)*						
		1994	1997	1994	1997	1994	1997
1.	Malnutrition rate (%)	30.0	23.8	17.4	12.2	44.7	37.3
	Literacy rate (%)	87.6	90.2	92.3	94.3	77.4	82.1
	[life expectancy (yrs.)]	--	68.0[1]	--	--	--	--
	[infant mort. (per 1,000 births)]	--	42.0[1]	--	--	--	--
2.	Poverty rate (%)[3]	53.5	49.0	46.1	40.4	67.0	64.7
	Poverty gap (%)	18.9	16.0	14.4	11.8	27.1	23.5
	Severe poverty rate (%)	18.8	14.8	12.9	9.3	29.5	24.5
3.	Consumption inequality, Gini	.360	.348	.351	.345	.349	.324
	Income inequality, Gini	.469	.484	.437	.441	.494	.500
	Wealth inequality, Gini	.695	.726	.672	.705	.706	.678
4.	Child labor[2] (%)	7.8	11.8	3.9	6.9	22.5	33.5
5.	School enrollment ('000)	4,880	5,080	2,960	3,030	1,920	2,050
	Public ambulatory Care (4 weeks, '000)	1,760	2,990	1,250	2,160	510	830
6.	Electricity connections (%)	68.8	73.7	93.7	97.4	23.2	30.3
	Sanitation connection (%)	48.2	58.6	73.4	84.3	2.4	11.6
	Water, public network (%)	65.0	72.8	84.9	89.0	28.8	43.1
	Homes with mud floors (%)	41.0	43.3	20.4	23.2	77.9	79.6

1	Life expectancy rate and infant mortality rate is for 1996.
2	Child labor: percent of all children, 6 to 14 years of age, working more than 15 hours per week.
3	See Annex Tables A2.6 and A2.7 for a regional breakdown of poverty statistics including the estimated standard errors.

Source: Staff estimates based on ENNIV (1994, 1997). Life expectancy and infant mortality rate for 1996 from World Bank (1998).

With respect to child labor we have to record a negative development. In 1997, more children were working (in both absolute numbers and percentages) than several years earlier. On the other hand, the public education and health sectors served more students and delivered more ambulatory care in 1997 than in 1994, although the rise of student enrollment rates in public primary and public secondary schools is very small. One cautionary remark is necessary here: the two household surveys on which we base our assessments were carried out in different months of the year, the 1994 survey in June/July and the 1997 survey in October/November. While this should not affect estimates of school enrollments since both periods are term times, health and illness patterns might be different. It would therefore be difficult to attribute the observed rise in ambulatory care treatments in health centers and hospitals to a larger and better public health service alone.

With respect to connection rates, the large public investments in basic infrastructure through programs such as FONCODES and FONAVI have increased these rates significantly. More than half a million households each have obtained sanitation, electricity, and public water. Electricity connections in urban areas are now almost complete; urban sanitation is at 85 percent (which still leaves 2.4 million urban residents without adequate hygiene facilities) and public water reaches 89 percent (with 1.7 million residents without water). Inroads in rural electrification and rural water have been made but gaps remain very large. Rural sanitation, although progressing as well, is still scarce. While public investments in infrastructure increased living standards of many families, the quality of existing housing stock itself does not seem to have improved. Actually, the percentage of dwellings with mud or earth floors have increased from 1994 to 1997, signaling that a substantial number of families constructing new dwellings - in urban and rural areas alike – do not have the resources to install a more hygienic and stable floor.

Comparisons. Some comparisons with other Latin American countries show that, despite the major improvements recorded above, Peru is still catching-up with respect to several of the recorded indicators. Graph 2 shows the infant mortality rate in 1996, setting it in relation to GNP per capita as recorded by the World Bank's Atlas method. Although Peru reduced infant mortality from 54 (1990) to 42

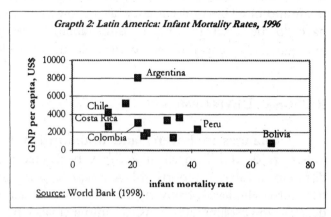

deaths per 1,000 live births in 1996, it is still lagging behind the regional achievements for countries of its income level and it places Peru among the worst in the Latin American region. Similarly, the maternal mortality rate for 1990-95 of 265 deaths for 100,000 births is almost one and half times higher than the LAC average and is 15 times the average of developed countries. For example, both Colombia and Costa Rica have considerably lower infant mortality rates (Colombia 25, Costa Rica 12) while they are roughly in the same income bracket than Peru. The same picture - although not as pronounced - can be seen for life expectancy. Here, it is estimated that Peru has a roughly four year lower life expectancy than its income level would suggest.[10] Such a gap does not exist for adult literacy where Peru performs according to expectations.

Similarly, access to basic services in Peru is still low despite the big successes achieved. Graph 3 shows Latin American countries and their per capita income level with respect to the percentage of the population having access to safe water. While the relationship is not as pronounced as in the case of the infant mortality rate, we can nevertheless also detect that Peru, with 72 percent water connection rates fares worse than Colombia or Mexico. Costa Rica - as in many instances - is the positive outlier.

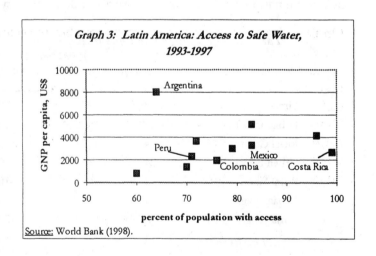

---

[10]   See Hicks and Peeters (1998).

Poverty rates are very difficult to compare internationally. As outlined in section 2 above, poverty estimates are based on household surveys, which differ considerably in sample design and content across countries. Many record only incomes and not consumption expenditures, which we use here for poverty measurement. Poverty lines are generally determined in national contexts, with varying goods baskets. Real prices, even after converting them into one common currency, also show wide variation so that purchasing power parities have to be used to obtain comparability. While efforts to make poverty statistics internationally comparable are worthwhile, they have to be handled with extreme care.[11]

REGIONAL DEVELOPMENTS

Changes in Poverty and Malnutrition Rates. While poverty and malnutrition indicators decreased in all of Peru's very diverse regions, rates of change have been quite different. Table 2 reports the *percentage of change* between 1994 and 1997; i.e., the table normalizes the level of poverty and malnutrition across regions. For example, a four percent decrease in absolute rates translates into a smaller percentage change in rural than urban Peru because the prevalence of poverty and malnutrition is much higher in rural areas. These percentage changes show that Peru made substantial inroads in reducing severe poverty and malnutrition.

However, the table also shows a stark urban-rural difference in these advances. Urban Peru was the driving force behind much of the gains for all three indicators. Two regions have performed better than the national average: the urban Sierra and Lima. On the other hand, the rural Sierra - where almost two-thirds of the total rural population live - has consistently performed worse than the national average. The one region where the indicators show an unusual trend is the rural Coast, where both poverty and severe poverty reduction rates are below the national average, but malnutrition declines very strongly.

Table 2: Percentage Changes in Regional Poverty and Malnutrition Rates, 1994-1997			
	Poverty	*Severe Poverty*	*Malnutrition*
Lima	-19	-25	-22
Urban Coast	+2	-23	-16
Rural Coast	-4	-13	-40
Urban Sierra	-24	-39	-42
Rural Sierra	-2	-16	-4
Urban Jungle	0	-23	-23
Rural Jungle	-7	-23	-26
Urban PERU	-13	-28	-30
Rural PERU	-4	-17	-17
Total Country	-8	-22	-21
<u>Source</u>: Staff Estimates based on ENNIV (1994, 1997).			

---

[11] In its *World Development Indicators* the World Bank used to include Peru in such international comparisons but, after reexamining the basic data, it has now stopped publishing estimated rates for the above reasons.

In accordance with these poverty and malnutrition reduction patterns, the developments over the past few have led to a higher concentration of deprivation in rural compared to urban areas of Peru. Graph 4 shows the distribution of the poor, severe poor and malnourished children below the age of five in 1994 and 1997. Almost 50 percent of the poor, 60 percent of the severe poor and 70 percent of the malnourished children lived in rural Peru in 1997. This occurs against the continuing urbanization of the country resulting in more than two-thirds of the population living in large and small cities.

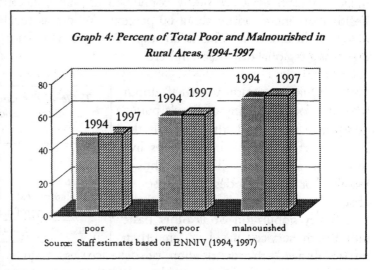

Graph 4: Percent of Total Poor and Malnourished in Rural Areas, 1994-1997

Source: Staff estimates based on ENNIV (1994, 1997)

Dispersion[12] in International Perspective. In line with the above, income per capita and consumption per capita differences across regions have increased, and Peru has an internationally high rate of internal regional dispersion. Per capita consumption in the urban Sierra and Lima increased by more than 15 percent while growth was negligible in the rural Sierra and even negative in the urban Selva (the jungle region) and urban Coast (Graph 5). By international standards, the existing regional dispersion in Peru is very high, as Table 3 shows. Peru has much higher inequalities than Colombia, Chile, Brazil, and even Mexico, and is only topped by Argentina.

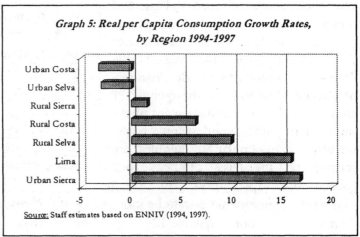

Graph 5: Real per Capita Consumption Growth Rates, by Region 1994-1997

Source: Staff estimates based on ENNIV (1994, 1997).

Table 3: Regional Dispersion Indicators, Latin American countries, various years

	Year	Dispersion
Argentina	1995	.736
Brazil	1994	.424
Chile	1994	.470
Colombia	1989	.358
Mexico	1993	.502
Peru	1997	.561

Source: Fallon (1998). Peru estimate from ENNIV (1997).

Distribution of New Social and Infrastructure Services. As Table 1 showed, basic and social service access rates increased strongly between 1994 and 1997. More than half a

---

[12] The dispersion indicator used here is the unweighted coefficient of variation (i.e. the standard deviation across regions divided by the national mean). See Fallon (1998).

million households were newly connected to water, electricity and sanitation. Ambulatory health visits increased by about 60 percent. Who was reached by the additional investments made in these areas? This is an important question for public policy, especially given the increasing regional dispersion in Peru.

Quite contrary to belief about the rural focus of many of Peru's public programs,[13] we find that by far the largest portion of new beneficiaries live in urban areas. As Table 4 shows, except for the (modest) increase in absolute school enrollment rates, the beneficiary population of all other basic and health services has been in urban areas.

Table 4: Distribution of New Access to Basic and Social Services, 1994-1997 (percentage)			
	Urban	Rural	
Water	57	43	(100)
Electricity	72	28	(100)
Sanitation	78	22	(100)
Ambulatory health	74	26	(100)
Education, enrollment	33	67	(100)
Source: Staff estimates based on ENNIV (1994, 1997).			

Indeed, the distribution of beneficiaries is quite close to the overall population distribution in Peru, which would suggest that expenditure distributions for these programs have largely been driven by population densities rather than poverty criteria.

Gains in new access to basic and social services were quite evenly distributed in the population and do not show a significant pro-poor bias. Table 5 shows new access by national population quintiles, with quintile 1 comprising the poorest 20 percent of the Peruvian population and quintile 5 the richest. The population quintiles are formed on the basis of per capita consumption expenditures. According

Table 5: Distribution of New Access to Basic and Social Services 1994-97, by population quintile			
water electricity		sanitation	health
1 (poorest)	20	18	18	16
2	25	25	24	20
3	21	18	20	18
4	18	20	18	26
5 (richest)	15	18	19	19
	(100)	(100)	(100)	(100)
Source: Staff estimates based on ENNIV (1994, 1997).			

to the results, programs seem to be more successful in reaching the poor in the second quintile than the severe poor in quintile 1.[14] In part, this is driven by the observed regional distribution of the additional expenditures. Obviously, these statistics on supply of services will translate into welfare gains for new beneficiaries only if the quality of the services is adequate. In an urban qualitative investigation conducted in 20 *centros poblados* (sub-district administrative units) by the Ministry of the Presidency in 1997, communities ranked the quality of water and sanitation services as their primary problem - while they had access, the services were not reliable.[15] Similarly, especially in the social sectors, the bottleneck in many localities might not be the *supply* of services but rather the *demand* of beneficiaries. The demand for health care, for

---

[13] See *Oxford Analytica* (1998).

[14] One important caveat has to be made here. Comparing quintiles between 1994 and 1997 in this way would assume that there is no mobility among population groups. As later pointed out, this is not the case. However, mobility is often restricted to movement to the closest quintile (e.g. from the bottom to the second quintile or from the richest to the fourth quintile). The overall assessment that infrastructure connections were distributed quite evenly across the population is therefore likely to hold.

[15] See Ministry of the Presidency (1997).

example, will be influenced by the costs of transport, waiting time, medicine and also by the compatibility of the offered services with traditional health beliefs.

INEQUALITY AND ITS COMPONENTS

After having detected that social and economic progress has not been evenly distributed in Peru, we now want to briefly return to the finding that, for the first time in a decade, inequality has risen in Peru. This section examines consumption, income, and wealth changes by quintile and then looks at the sources of this rising inequality.

Consumption, Income and Wealth Growth Rates. Consumption, income, and wealth changes reveal a quite different distribution of gains in prosperity. Graph 6 shows that per capita consumption changes were highest for the poorest and richest quintiles. While true also for income changes, gains were clearly tilted toward the richest quintile, as reflected in the rise in income inequality reported above.

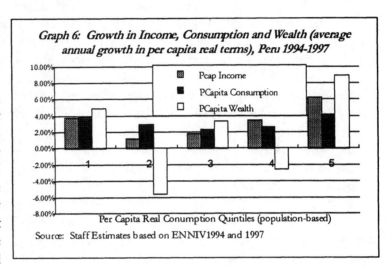

Graph 6: Growth in Income, Consumption and Wealth (average annual growth in per capita real terms), Peru 1994-1997

Source: Staff Estimates based on ENNIV 1994 and 1997

Changes in wealth of these same population groups show a wide variation, which might be due in part to changes in reporting behavior. However, according to these estimates the richest quintile again records the highest per capita growth rates of wealth[16], thus increasing wealth inequality. [17] It is not uncommon to find that consumption and income inequality show different trends – most importantly, income differs from consumption by including savings (or dissavings). Since such savings will determine the distribution of assets and wealth in the long run, economists generally tend to assign income inequality developments more weight than developments in consumption inequality.

These results are confirmed by a different data source: examining income inequality changes between 1995 and 1997, the Peruvian Statistical Institute (INEI) finds the Gini coefficient increasing as well. According to preliminary estimates based on the large National Household Survey (*Encuestas Nacional de Hogares*), the Gini coefficient increased between 1995 and 1997[18], thus supporting the findings presented here.

---

[16]   The wealth variable includes the value of consumer durable goods, the value of owned houses (self-assessment), and the value of property and equipment. The wealth changes reported in the graph correspond to population quintiles defined using household per capita expenditures.

[17]   See Annex 2 for a definition of income. In accordance with the definition of consumption, the income variable does not include the rental value of the house because the question on rental value was changed in the 1997 questionnaire.

[18]   Communication with MECOVI project staff, INEI.

Sources of the rise in inequality. What are the contributing factors behind this increase in wealth and income inequality? We first look at the impact of the different components of income. What would happen if one of the components of income were to increase? Does this lower or increase inequality? Table 6 reports the impact on total inequality from increasing income of each component by one percent: income from self-employment (comprising microenterprise owners, professionals, and entrepreneurs) reduces inequality strongly (by almost 5 percent), while all other categories - wage income, transfers and income from property - tend to increase inequality. The rise in inequality in Peru over the three years can be largely attributed to a declining share of self-employment income and rising shares of transfer and property income.

Table 6: Expected Changes in Income Inequality by Income Source, 1997 (percent of Gini change)

Income source	Expected Change
Self-employment income	-4.9
Wages	0.6
Transfers	2.2
property income	2.1

Source: Rodriguez (1998).

Repeating the exercise for wealth, the driving forces behind wealth inequality are housing and urban property (Table 7). Wealth is defined here as the total value of housing, durable goods (resale value), urban property, agricultural property, and enterprises. Increasing each of the components by one percent - while leaving all the others constant - would increase the Gini coefficient in the case of housing and urban property while decreasing it if wealth from durable consumer goods or agricultural property were to increase. Hence, it appears that land distribution and the allocation of durable goods among households is more equal than the overall wealth distribution in the country.

Table 7: Expected Changes in Wealth Inequality by Wealth Source, 1997 (percent of Gini change)

Wealth source	Expected Change
Housing	1.9
Durable goods	-1.5
Urban property	1.3
Agricultural property	-1.6
Enterprises	0

Source: Rodriguez (1998).

There are two variables associated with the observed rises in income inequality: education and regional income differences. First, the more educated Peruvians profited more from the current upswing than the less educated. This reflects a finding common to many analyses over the past few years, i.e., that incomes of the highly educated are rising by more than the incomes of the less educated. Average incomes of families with higher education rose by 63 percent between 1994 and 1997, while average incomes of those with primary education or less rose by just 5 percent. Obviously, this does not mean that new investment in education would increase inequality further – quite the contrary, improving the quality of primary and secondary education would decrease inequality. Second, - and as already outlined above, - the widening of inter-regional differences has contributed to a rise in inequality as well.

What types of policies would help to reduce income and wealth inequality? First, education and training of the less educated and their children would help equality. Second, a balanced regional pattern of growth would do the same. Here, it might be interesting to think about the role of provincial and local governments in promoting more equitable regional development. Lastly, policies that improve income-earning possibilities from self-employment - such as micro-enterprises – would also tend to lower inequality.

International Comparisons. While we have cautioned against direct comparisons of poverty rates across countries, a stronger case can, however, be made to compare distribution

16

statistics across countries because these do not depend on the fixing of some real baseline, as is the case with an absolute poverty line. Table 8 shows that Latin American income inequality is the highest is the world, even higher than for Sub-Saharan Africa. While Peru's inequality, measured by the Gini coefficient, was above the Latin American average in the 1970s and 1980s, this appears to have changed in the 1990s. There is quite general agreement that income inequality in Peru decreased from the mid-1980s to the mid-1990s.[19]

Table 8: Inequality by Region (Gini coefficients, multiplied by 100)				
	1960s	1970s	1980s	1990s
Eastern Europe	25.1	24.6	25.0	28.9
OECD and high income	35.0	34.8	33.2	33.8
East Asia/Pacific	37.4	39.9	38.7	38.1
South Asia	36.2	34.0	35.0	31.9
Middle East/North Africa	41.4	41.9	40.5	38.0
Sub-Saharan Africa	49.9	48.2	43.5	47.0
Latin America	53.2	49.1	49.8	49.3
Peru	**n/a**	**55.0**	**51.8**	**47.2**

Sources: IMF (1998, p.2). Peru's rates for 1980s (=1985) from Saavedra and Diaz (1997), for 1990s (=average 1994 and 1997) from Rodriguez (1998).

However, in the period from 1994 to 1997, income inequality was on the rise for the first time since 1985-86, very close to the Latin American average with a Gini coefficient of 48.5. Graph 7 shows the latest estimates of income inequality in Latin American countries. Peru has considerably more equality than Brazil, Colombia, and also Mexico but less than Costa Rica, Venezuela, and Bolivia.

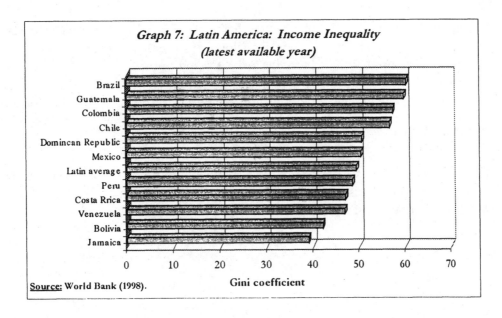

Graph 7: Latin America: Income Inequality (latest available year)

Gini coefficient

Source: World Bank (1998).

---

[19] See Saavedra and Diaz (1997) and Escobal et al (1998). Contrary to the above data shown, Londoño and Székely (1997) find that, overall, income inequality in Latin America increased significantly during the 1980s but that inequality has subsequently *not* decreased.

4.   POVERTY - CHANGING FACES?

This section looks at how different groups in society have fared over the past years and how - if at all - the main factors linked to poverty have changed. Whenever possible, we will also make reference to some of the other welfare indictors looked at in the previous section; however, data limitations will restrict us to concentrating largely on consumption poverty.

We will abstain from presenting a full poverty profile in this section - much has been written and is by now well understood about the main causes and correlates of poverty in Peru.[20] To briefly summarize, nevertheless: compared to better-off groups, the poor continue to live in worse and smaller dwellings, generally with adobe walls and earth floors. They have less access to markets, especially in rural areas, and their possessions are limited; almost all of the urban poor have access to radios, most to TVs, but only one in five families has a telephone. With few exceptions, there are no telephones at all in rural Peru. Electricity connections in the cities are almost universal but only about a fifth of the rural poor can rely on electricity for lighting. Poor city dwellers still have to cook with kerosene; the rural poor - if they can - rely on wood. About 40 percent of the poor can't afford to see a doctor or nurse when they are sick. With health access, especially in rural areas, still sparse, transportation, waiting and medicine costs are simply too high and only ten percent of the poor are covered by some form of health insurance. Finally, education still is one of the main driving forces behind welfare differences in Peru - looking at the average years of education, poor household heads in urban areas have about 6.5 years of formal training and non-poor heads 9 years. Educational attainment in rural Peru is even lower and so is the gap between groups: for poor household heads 4.5 years (less than needed to finish primary school) and for non-poor ones 6 years (or barely attendance of secondary school).

Instead of describing static differences in living conditions, we are interested here how *poverty risks* have changed over time. That is, by belonging to a specific group in society, e.g. an age group or ethnic group, how high was the risk of being poor in 1994? And how did this risk change over time; did it increase or decrease? Such an analysis will help us to identify relative trends, e.g., has the indigenous population caught up to the developments for the non-indigenous groups? Or has the gap between them increased and their degree of economic exclusion widened?

The selection of these risks and their relative importance follows an analysis of hundreds of *identical* households in 1994 and 1997 (see Box 1 and Annex 1). This allows us to single out the most important factors determining welfare changes.

---

[20]   See, for example, Moncada and Webb (1996).

Examining how 900 identical households fared between 1994 and 1997 sheds light on the determinants of household welfare dynamics. As Annex 1 describes in more detail, we studied the determining factors of per capita consumption growth. Results indicate that:

a.   *Female-headed households had higher per capita growth rates than male-headed households;*

b.   *Migrant families did nor fare worse than non-migrant families;*

c.   *Native language speakers clearly fell behind.* One of the strongest results is related to language, and with it ethnicity. Even when we control for other variables that are correlated with language, such as geographic location, native language-speaking households still fall further behind Spanish-speaking households;

d.   *Infrastructure is of major importance and we find increasing returns to services.* We find evidence of increasing returns to the number of services that households command. Hence, a household with four services (telephone, water, electricity, and sanitation) obtains more than double the welfare improvement than households with two services. Looking at services by type, electricity is the most important service linked to household welfare improvements in rural areas, while a telephone appears to be the most important service in urban areas;

e.   *Access to savings increase per capita growth rates;*

f.   *Household size impacts welfare.* We find that household size significantly influences welfare dynamics. Larger households fare worse than smaller ones, as larger households also tend to have higher dependency ratios (ratio of income to non-income earning members of household). With higher dependency ratios households may to save less leading to lower welfare changes over time.

g.   *Better education and more experience means faster advance.* The higher the education of the household head in 1994, the larger the growth in per capita expenditures;

h.   *Households with home-based businesses or off-farm employment opportunities fare better.* Both urban and rural households that use at least one room in the house for business purposes achieved significantly higher growth of welfare than households that do not. Closely linked to this, we find some evidence that households with the head of the household employed in the informal sector definitely did not do worse (but rather better) than households with the head employed in the formal sector.

POVERTY COMPARISONS - HOW DID GROUPS IN SOCIETY FARE?

This section takes a closer look at a number of different groups in society that have, in the past, been identified as particularly poor. These include the native-speaking population and we use language here as a corollary of ethnicity, children of different ages, adolescents, women-headed households, rural widow-headed households, migrants and the landless. Our main aims are to see whether members of these groups are particularly at risk of being poor and whether group characteristics are important in the changes in this risk. While we will briefly touch on other dimensions of well-being, such as political and social integration, we will limit ourselves mainly to this material view of poverty.

Table 9 reports poverty risks for each group relative to the other members of society. A positive entry means that the population belonging to this group is *more* likely to be poor than the rest of the population; a negative entry stands for the reverse. Hence, these are not *absolute* poverty rates but *relative* ones compared to all other groups. The last column of the table shows the share of the total poor population in Peru belonging to this group. The latter is important for policymakers as the poverty risk might be extremely high for a group in the population but they might represent only a tiny fraction of the total poor population.

Table 9: Relative Poverty Risks of Selected Groups -- More or Less Likely to be Poor? (percent)

	National 1994	1997	Percent Total Poor, 1997
Native language speakers	+40.2	+48.7	[20.9]
Children, 0-5 years	+26.2	+27.4	[18.4]
Children, 6-14 years	+24.6	+25.3	[15.5]
Youth, 15-17 years	+ 5.3	+ 8.6	[6.7]
Rural households, landless	+ 3.5	-3.7	[16.2]
Rural widow-headed households	-5.1	-14.2	[2.5]
Female headed households	-12.8	-16.5	[10.7]
Migrants	-16.3	-17.8	[28.2]

Source: Staff estimates based on ENNIV (1994, 1997). The entries in the table are simple relative poverty risks and do not take into account the influence of other variables. Regression results from the panel data analysis, which guided us in the selection of variables, are included in Box 1 (see also Annex I). Poverty rates, as in the whole report, are based on consumption per capita.

Native-speaking Population. The native-speaking population[21] is, of all the groups considered here, the one with the highest relative poverty risk, and we find this risk increasing - which implies that the native-speaking population is falling further behind the Spanish-speaking population. We use language as a proxy for indigeneity because indigeneity cannot be defined - indigenous languages, traditional clothing, heritage, and observed traditions and beliefs can, but need not, be part of the life of indigenous people. Accordingly, estimates of the indigenous population vary between 10 and 40 percent of the population. However, with language being an integral part of indigenous culture, we employ it here as a proxy for indigeneity. We find that the native-speaking population was 40 percent more likely to be poor than the Spanish-speaking population in 1994 and 49 percent more likely to be poor in 1997 - in other words, native speakers are falling behind. Native language was also one of the most robust and important factors when we examined welfare changes of several hundred identical households between 1994 and 1997 (see Box 1) - controlling for everything else (e.g. education, geographic location, experience, household size), the native-language speaking families had significantly lower consumption growth rates than the Spanish-speaking population.

Integration of the indigenous population has long been recognized as one of the most important challenges in the fight against poverty and deprivation in Peru. Education levels of

---

[21] We classify all those households as native-speaking for which the household head reported that her or his mother tongue is Quechua, Aymara, Campa or another native language. See MacIsaac and Patrinos (1995) or Davis and Patrinos (1996).

adults are low and illiteracy levels are still substantial (21 percent of the rural native speaking population above 6 years old are illiterate). School attendance of indigenous children is significantly below the national average, and children from indigenous families are more than twice as likely to be malnourished than children from a non-indigenous background. Other factors such as education or experience being equal, native language speakers earn less income.[22] Due in part to the fact that the majority of the native-language speaking population lives in rural areas, its access to electricity, sanitation, water, and health services is lower than for the Spanish-speaking population.

Examining the distribution of *new* access to basic and social services from 1994 to 1997 in rural areas, success in reaching the native-speaking population was mixed. Only new sanitation investments went mostly to native speakers. All others, and especially water and ambulatory hospital care, reached mainly the non-indigenous population. These figures are particularly significant in light of the composition of the extreme poor were native speakers in 1997: almost 60 percent of the extreme poor were native speakers.

Table 10: Distribution of New Access to Rural Basic and Social Services, by Language, 1994-1997 (percentage)		
New access	Native Speakers	Non-Native Speakers
Water connection	22	78 (100)
Electricity connection	47	53 (100)
Sanitation services	60	40 (100)
Ambulatory care, hospital	23	77 (100)
Ambulatory care, prim. clinic	48	52 (100)
memo:		
Dist. of severe poor	60	40 (100)
Dist. of rural poor	48	52 (100)
Rural Population	42	58 (100)
Source: Staff estimates based on ENNIV (1994, 1997).		

The above suggests that the Government of Peru needs to take a careful look at its attempts to reach one of the most deprived groups in the country, its indigenous population. With 60 percent of the severe poor in rural areas being native speakers and the massive public investments over the three years under study having had only limited success in reaching them, one possibility would be to try to bring in groups that have long worked in and with isolated, poor communities as partners in the poverty reduction effort. The Ministry of the Presidency in its *Lucha contra la Pobreza* (fight against poverty) has attempted such a partnership approach, especially in rural areas, and now works closely with a number of respected and knowledgeable NGOs to facilitate, plan, and implement community-based projects. While an evaluation of this approach remains to be carried out, it does represent an innovative and very promising way to channeling much-needed help to the severe poor indigenous population.

Children. In the age distribution, children are the poorest group in Peruvian society. More precisely, many children live in poor households, since we define poverty at the household level.[23] Children below 14 years old had a 25 percent higher risk of being poor

---

[22] MacIsaac and Patrinos (1995). See also Lopez and della Maggiora (1998, p.20-21), who find that, controlling for other factors, native background reduces income of farmers and non-farm workers by 44 percent. They report, though, that this difference disappears after controlling for village effects, which could be a proxy for geographic isolation.

[23] Household surveys contain very limited information about the intra-household distribution of resources. Hence, if a household is poor then all of its members are assumed to be poor although this need not be true. Similarly, depending on the intra-household resources distribution, 'non-poor' households might have

than the rest of the population and this relative risk slightly increased over the three years. We also find a rather worrying trend when looking at child labor rates (Table 11): these doubled for children between 6 and 14. Child labor is much higher in the poorer segments of society. Almost one out of four severely poor children worked more than 10 hours per week in 1997. Both of these trends point to children remaining a particularly vulnerable group in society.[24]

Table 11: Child Labor, 1994 and 1997 (percent of children ages 6 to 14)				
	more than 15 hours per week		more than 10 hours per week	
quintile	1994	1997	1994	1997
1	11.9	16.7	17.5	24.3
2	7.7	13.1	11.9	21.1
3	7.4	10.1	9.2	16.3
4	6.4	9.2	8.7	14.3
5	2.0	6.1	4.3	8.5
total	7.8	11.8	11.3	18.1
no. ('000)	375	616	549	940

Source: Staff estimates based on ENNIV (1994, 1997).

On the positive side, malnutrition rates have declined strongly, by both region and gender. Table 12 shows that malnutrition in the rural Sierra remains very high; almost every second child is malnourished. A qualitative and quantitative inquiry by Caritas (1997) in selected Sierra communities confirmed the high prevalence of malnutrition. Girls remain slightly more at risk of being malnourished than boys, but the gender gap appears to be closing slowly. Preliminary results from examining the determinants of malnutrition rates confirm earlier analyses in Peru: the main determinants are the poverty level (household consumption) and

Table 12: Malnutrition Rates by Region and Gender, 1994 and 1997 (percent of children below age 5)		
quintile	1994	1997
Lima	12.1	9.0
Urb. Coast	12.1	10.0
Rur. Coast	32.4	20.1
Urb. Sierra	27.9	14.7
Rur. Sierra	47.9	45.7
Urb. Jungle	28.7	23.4
Rural Jungle	44.7	36.4
Total girls	31.6	24.8
Total boys	28.8	22.9
Total country	30.1	23.8

Source: Staff Estimates based on ENNIV 1994 and 1997.

educational status of the mother. Access to basic services such as clean water, sanitation, and electricity corresponds with decreasing malnutrition levels.

Youth. The third age group we find at increasing relative risk of poverty is adolescents. While they were about 5 percent more likely to be poor than all other age groups in 1994, they were 8.6 percent more likely to be poor in 1997 (see Table 9). Adolescents are of particular concern, especially in urban areas, for two additional reasons: first, it is the only age group for which unemployment rates remain very high - for all other age groups, open

Table 13: Unemployment Rates by gender, Metropolitan Lima, 1992-1996				
	1993	1994	1995	1996
male				
14-18 yrs	19.4	12.1	14.9	18.2
Total male	10.0	9.0	7.1	7.2
female				
14-18 yrs	21.0	11.8	11.4	13.9
Total female	12.4	12.0	8.7	8.5

Source: Encuesta de Hogares, Ministry of Labor, and Saavedra (1998).

poor members as well. The discussion about child poverty should therefore be more precisely framed as "children living in poor families".

[24] See also Rodriguez and Abler (1998). They find the result that child labor in Peru tends to be pro-cyclical, i.e., falling with an economic downturn and increasing with an economic boom.

unemployment dropped after the recovery started at the beginning of the 1990s. As shown in Table 13, unemployment rates increased substantially for both female and male adolescents between 1995 and 1996 in Lima. Second, the young are also increasingly involved in violent acts. A recent survey by the Statistical Institute INEI shows that young people are held responsible for 90 percent of acts of vandalism and about 25 percent of acts of physical violence.

Landless. Anthropological studies generally indicate that the rural landless population is a particularly poor group. According to the household surveys, however, while the landless rural households were slightly more likely to be poor than the rural households owning land in 1994, this relative risk has disappeared in the past several years (Table 9). Sociological studies point out, though, that the impact of landlessness might not show up in official data, since households led by the elderly or widows often do not have the physical strength to work their own land after the previous head of the household has migrated or died. These would be de facto landless households (although not identified as such) as they do not derive income from farming their land. [25] We tested this assertion by computing the relative risk of rural widow-headed households being poor (Table 9). It appears that these households, astonishingly, fare better in relative terms to other rural households and that their relative risk of poverty decreased over the years.

Gender. Viewed from many different angles, gender gaps in Peru seem to be closing. First, households with female heads have fared better than male headed households over the last years. Their relative risk of poverty is considerably lower and continues to decline. Similarly, when examining which group of households did well over the three years, we found that female headship - controlling for all

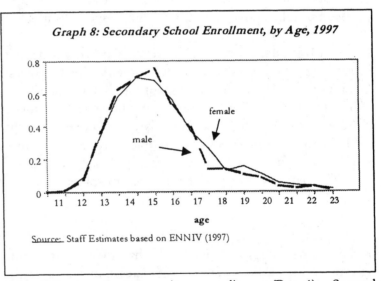

Graph 8: Secondary School Enrollment, by Age, 1997

Source: Staff Estimates based on ENNIV (1997)

other factors - had a strong positive influence on per capita expenditures (Box 1). Second, labor market discrimination (i.e. women earning less than men although they have the same education, experience, and age) has disappeared in the urban formal and informal sectors.[26] However, women continue be disadvantaged is rural non-farm employment.[27] Third, malnutrition rates are not equal yet between boys and girls but the gap is slowly narrowing as well. Finally, regarding education, of most concern in the past was secondary school enrollment of girls. Graph 8, which shows the percentage of secondary school attendance by

---

[25]   See, for example, Luerssen (1993).

[26]   Saavedra and Chong (1999).

[27]   Lopez and della Maggiora (1998).

age group of the population, also confirms that, at least in terms of school attendance, there is now almost no difference between boys and girls. Participation rates in the labor force do remain considerably lower for women than for men. Increases, however, are faster for women.

Briefly looking at the role of women at high levels of power and decisionmaking, women account for about 11 percent of seats in parliament, 20 percent of administrators, and 40 percent of professional and technical workers. Although still far behind men, women's role in politics and management in Peru is about comparable to that of its neighbors (Table 14). Peru does lag behind other Latin American countries regarding the role of women as professional technical workers, though. Also - as explored below in more detail - a new problem of urban poverty, social violence, especially affects women.

	seats held in parliament (% women)	administrators & managers (% women)	prof. & tech. workers (% women)
Bolivia	6.4	16.8	41.9
Brazil	6.7	17.3	57.2
Colombia	9.8	27.2	41.8
Costa Rica	15.8	21.1	44.9
Mexico	13.9	20.0	43.6
Peru	10.8	20.0	41.1
Uruguay	6.9	25.3	62.6
Venezuela	6.3	17.6	55.2

Table 14: Women at High Levels of Power and Decisionmaking

Source: United Nations (1997a).

Migrants. Based on the relative risk of being poor, migrant families appear to be integrating well into their new environment. Such families were at 16 percent lower risk of being poor in 1994 than non-migrant families and at 18 percent lower risk in 1997 (Table 9). While most rural-to-urban migrants state that they migrate for income and employment reasons, their educational level tends to be higher than that of non-migrant families, which explains their relatively good economic integration in cities to which they migrated.[28] Also, migration is one of the strongest factors linking the rural and often indigenous countryside with the generally *mestizo* cities because migrants maintain their rural links and community networks.[29]

Internally Displaced. One group often considered at a very high risk of deprivation is the internally displaced people who had to leave their rural residence for reasons of political violence. The United Nations estimates that still today, years after the marked decline of political violence, about half a million Peruvians are internally displaced.[30] These are especially rural-rural migrants who have had to leave their house, land, and family networks and have not (yet) returned to their original place of residence. To help families resettle to their homes, the Peruvian Government created the *Proyecto de Apoyo al Reboplamineto y Desarrollo de Zonas de Emergencia* (PAR) in 1993. By the year 2000, the program plans to have helped a total of one million internally displaced persons.

---

[28] See Escobal et al (1998) and White et al (1995).

[29] Altamirano (1988).

[30] United Nations (1997b).

We now turn from a focus on groups to a recap of factors that underlie poverty changes. Obviously, these two categories are often intrinsically interlinked. The native-speaking population, for example, is at a higher relative risk of poverty than the Spanish-speaking population, partly because their education attainments are lower, their access to markets is scarcer, and their dependency ratios are higher. The factors analyzed below, however, are significant independently of - or better, in addition to - looking at different groups in society. Again, their selection is based mainly on the examination of hundreds of identical households over time and relating the change in their welfare level (consumption per capita growth) to household and individual member characteristics. Table 15 reports the *relative* risks of poverty for such factors. As above, the interpretation of the data is relative to the rest of the population.

Table 15: Poverty Risks of Selected Factors -- More or Less Likely to be Poor? (population percentages)	National 1994	National 1997	Percent of Total Poor, 1997
Households using house for business purposes	-28.2	-29.0	[10.9]
Rural households with at least one member in off-farm empl.	-24.0	-22.7	[18.2]
Households with spouse or partner of head working	-10.8	-20.6	[35.6]
Households without water and sanitation	+54.2	+49.5	[35.7]
Households without electricity	+63.0	+68.5	[37.6]
Households with head less than secondary education	+72.8	+72.3	[61.7]
Households of 7 persons or more	+71.4	+106.4	[31.7]

1   spouse working is defined in remunerated work in the last seven days before the survey was conducted.

Source: Staff estimates based on ENNIV (1994, 1997). The entries in the table are simple relative poverty risks and do not take into account the influence of other variables. Regression results from the panel data analysis, which guided us in the selection of variables, are included in Box 1. Poverty rates, as in the whole report, are based on consumption per capita.

Houses Used for Business Purposes.   In both 1994 and 1997, Peruvians living in households that were able to use at least part of their house for some income-generating activity were almost 30 percent less likely to be poor than the population not having such an income possibility. And this was one of the very robust and strong factors which we found helped families *advance* over the last years (Annex 1). Such businesses can be formal (e.g., a formal store in the house, professionals working from home), but in the large majority of cases are informal. Renting out a room, performing home-based piecework, selling merchandise out of the house, or small manufacturing on a sub-contract basis would fall under this category.

To the degree that legal home ownership is related to the home being used for business purposes, the current drive to provide titles for urban dwellings in Peru can indeed be of major importance for the poor. Home ownership in Peru is very large, with about three out of four families living in their own houses. This, interestingly, does not vary much with the poverty level of families. However, many of the poor, especially in Lima, who invaded their land in the big migration flow at the end of the 1980s and beginning of the 1990s, do not have legal title to their property. If, as found in several qualitative and quantitative studies,[31] legal

---

31   See, for example, Moser (1996) and Persaud (1992).

home ownership encourages home investment and this raises the likelihood of using the home as an income-generating asset, the current urban property drive can have very positive poverty effects.

The finding that such informal businesses can be important for helping families advance is in line with a rather positive, or at least neutral, view of the informal sector in Peru. Informality remains huge, accounting for almost half of urban employment. However, for the self-employed who open microenterprises, informal sector employment in Peru is largely a *choice*. People are not forced into informality by distortionary policies or labor market practices. Those policies were dismantled to a very large extent at the beginning of the 1990s. The main reason for remaining in the informal sector in self-employment is entrepreneurial skill.[32] Confirming this view of the informal sector in Peru, households whose head was employed in the informal sector had a *higher* per capita growth rate of consumption than household heads working in the formal sector even when we control for other factors. For informal wage earners the picture is different. Here, segmentation still exists - i.e., given their education, experience and other individual characteristics, wage earners in the informal sector are earning less than they would in the formal sector. Such workers tend to be young, and single, not heads of households. Hence, it is suggested that they lack experience and are in a waiting position to find formal sector employment.

Services. Households without basic services such as water, electricity, sanitation, and telephones are at a much higher relative risk of being poor than households that command these services. Obviously, we will find a mutual dependence between poverty level and services access: poorer households tend to be located in poorer neighborhoods so that the likelihood of them having access is low. Simply stating that access is lower does not imply that there is a causal link with poverty. However, in the panel analysis of identical households, we found very strong evidence that households that had access to basic services in 1994 had a significantly higher growth rate of per capita consumption than households that did not have such access. Many reasons for this can be found, such as a positive impact on health through clean water supply and sanitation services or the importance for home enterprises of electricity and phone connections.

Furthermore, the bundling of services is very important for households. The additional positive impact of each new service increases with the total number of services available. Based on the analysis of the household panel, we show in Graph 9 that adding a fourth service has about seven times a higher additional impact than linking a second service to households. Hence, · the joint provision of services is important to realize welfare effects: for example,

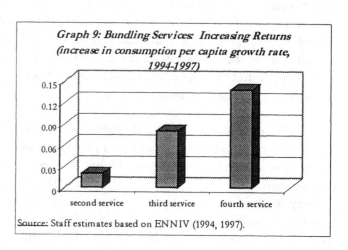

Graph 9: Bundling Services: Increasing Returns (increase in consumption per capita growth rate, 1994-1997)

Source: Staff estimates based on ENNIV (1994, 1997).

---

[32]   See Saavedra and Chong (1999) and Yamada (1996).

clean water access will improve household's well-being more if it comes *together* with sanitation. Health risks might decline with water access but the real benefit might only materialize if the services are provided together.

The positive impact of such bundled, integrated interventions in Peru has been observed in a different study. In a recent study, electrification and sanitation services were found to increase the returns to education significantly in rural and urban Peru alike - as children can read and study longer at night, they profit more from schooling. Sanitation is likely to lower illness and malnutrition and have a positive effect on learning. Also, better rural roads and rural transport were shown to have a very positive impact on the returns to rural education.[33]

Education. Educational attainment remains not only one of the central determining factors of poverty levels, but it also determines who advances rapidly or falls behind in the Peruvian society. In Table 15, we see that in 1994 Peruvians living in an household whose head had less than secondary education were 70 percent more likely to be poor than the rest of the population. This huge relative risk stayed constant until 1997, but the panel study showed that the higher the initial education of the household head, the higher was per capita consumption growth: the better educated have

Table 16: Urban Peru: Educational Premia, 1991 and 1996 (percent)			
	1991	*1996*	*change*
Primary/ no education	40.0	33.0	-7.0
Secondary/ primary	7.0	17.0	10.0
Non-university higher/secondary	13.0	25.0	12.0
University/non-university higher	47.0	70.0	33.0
Source: Saavedra (1998).			

benefited proportionately more than the less educated in recent years. This is in line with many findings in Peru that not only have returns to education increased across the board since the beginning of the 1990s but that they have increased *more* for those with better education. Table 16 shows education premia (i.e., the difference in income levels according to educational attainment) for urban Peru in 1991 and 1996. Educational premia increased most strongly for university-educated Peruvians, and hence was one of the driving forces behind the increase in inequality over the past years. As a side note, Peru's returns to education are not below those observed in other Latin America countries. And together with Colombia, Chile, Argentina, and Costa Rica, education returns have increased during the period of structural reforms.

Enrollment in secondary school, its quality, and financing remains a matter of concern in the education sector. Both primary and secondary school enrollment rates have increased steadily since the beginning of the decade, and gaps in enrollment rates by poverty level have disappeared for school beginners. Differences in school attendance remain for secondary

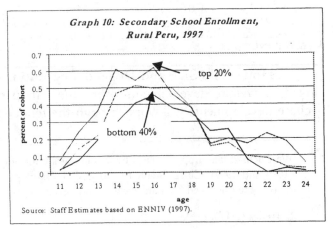

Graph 10: Secondary School Enrollment, Rural Peru, 1997

top 20%

bottom 40%

percent of cohort

age

Source: Staff Estimates based on ENNIV (1997).

---

[33] See Escobal et al (1998).

school, especially in rural areas, as Graph 10 shows: for the poorest group (bottom quintile of the population), enrollment rates are still considerably lower than for children from well-off families. Quality indicators show that much remains to be improved in the sector: a large difference between net and gross enrollment rates indicates that many children are in primary and secondary school longer than they should be. And dropout rates in secondary school have increased between 1994 and 1997. Table 17 shows this increase and also the continuing, very strong link between dropout rates and poverty levels.[34]

Although having increased by 30 percent in real terms from 1994 to 1997, education expenditures are still low in historical perspective and highly tilted toward the more well-off regions of the country. It is estimated that educational per capita expenditures in 1997 were roughly 20 percent below their 1970 level.[35] And these per capita expenditures are significantly higher in better-off departments. Graph 11 plots

quintile	Urban		Rural	
	1994	1997	1994	1997
1	11.0	22.0	14.0	27.0
2	8.0	18.0	15.0	22.0
3	6.0	8.0	13.0	9.0
4	4.0	8.0	15.0	11.0
5	3.0	4.0	15.0	4.0

Table 17: Drop-Out Rates in Secondary School, 1994 and 1997 (percent)

Source: Staff estimates based on ENNIV (1994,1997).

per capita student expenditures by department against the FONCODES poverty index; the poorer the department, the lower the per student educational expenditures. Such a spending pattern perpetuates regional and general inequality in Peru.

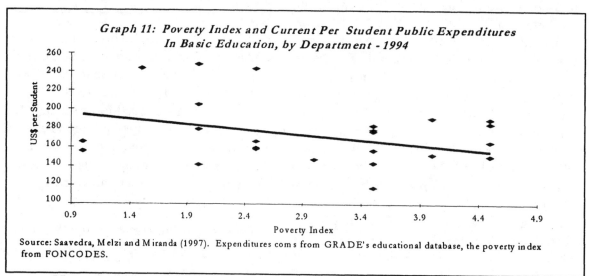

Graph 11: Poverty Index and Current Per Student Public Expenditures In Basic Education, by Department - 1994

Source: Saavedra, Melzi and Miranda (1997). Expenditures coms from GRADE's educational database, the poverty index from FONCODES.

Household Size and Dependency Ratio. We find that household size is negatively linked to welfare developments over time. In part, the link between household size and welfare developments will work through the tendency that larger households also have more

---

[34] We calculate the drop out rates by looking at a constant age cohort, the 16 to 19 year olds in both years (1994 and 1997). Since Graph 10 shows that a large percentage of that age cohort still attends secondary school, the calculated rates are likely to underestimate the true dropout rates.

[35] Saavedra (1998).

dependents per income earner. Such a higher dependency ratio will likely mean that households cannot save much of their current income for the future and consume most of it at present. Their future earning and consumption possibilities are hence reduced.

Off-farm Employment. Off-farm employment, although still very thin, has the potential to be a road out of poverty in rural areas. We find that the likelihood of being poor was about 24 percent lower for rural families that had at least one member in off-farm activities in 1994 and about 23 percent lower in 1997 (Table 15). Also, in the panel study of households, off-farm employment influenced consumption growth of households strongly and positively. The labor market, though, comprised of trade, small-scale manufacturing, and transport remains relatively unimportant in comparison to agricultural employment: in 1994, only about 13 percent of total workday equivalents were devoted to off-farm labor activities in rural Peru. This is considerably lower than in other countries in the region.[36] The strong link we find between off-farm activities and welfare improvements of households points to a potential role for these activities in the fight against poverty. Studies from other countries have shown that, in addition to general economic performance, rural off-farm activities depend heavily on infrastructure, especially rural roads.

Urban Violence. Urban violence is one of the biggest preoccupations of the urban poor. Although acts of political violence have been contained since the beginning of this decade, public concern about criminal and social forms of violence - including robberies, armed attacks, and sexual assaults - has risen sharply in recent times, as mirrored by the attention they receive in the media. How important violence, its different forms, and its impacts are for the life of the urban population is shown by the outcome of a ranking exercise. The Ministry of the Presidency asked 20 poor neighborhoods in the Lima district of Ate[37] (with a sample of almost 40,000

Rank #	Problem	Problem in # of communities
1	water & sewerage: not working	17
2	child malnutrition	15
3	street conditions bad/accidents	15
4	violence (assaults, domestic)	14
5	houses: unfinished	· 14
6	environmental pollution and related contagious diseases	14
7	no employment	12
8	distance to basic education	9
9	no local community hall	8
10	youth gangs	8
11	bad basic health care	7
12	insecure land ownership	6
13	no recreational space	5
14	*vaso de leche* program not well equipped	3
15	drugs, alcohol	3

Table 18: Urban Problems: Ranking Exercise of Twenty Communities in Ate, Lima, December 1997

Source: Ministry of the Presidency (1997).

people) to conduct neighborhood meetings in which the main problems of the population would be prioritized, their main causes identified and possible solutions suggested. Each

---

[36]   See Saavedra (1998) and Lanjouw (1998).

[37]   Ate is a big district in Lima's eastern cone. It has almost 300,000 inhabitants and according to the FONCODES poverty map (derived from the census), about half of its population has no connection to water or sewerage, and 30 percent are without (legal) electricity connections. The malnutrition rate of minors below the age of five, extrapolated using census data, is about 30 percent. About half of the houses were in the 'vivienda precaria' category. School assistance rates are very high (95%) and analfabetism 5.1 percent. These indicators, aggregated into one index used by FONCODES, rank Ate as the tenth poorest district in Lima (out of 41).

community could specify as many problems as it deemed important. Table 18 records the consolidated results of all 20 case studies.

Violence was one of the main problems identified by these twenty urban communities. As shown in Table 18, fourteen communities specified assaults, robberies, and domestic violence as one of their largest problems, after water and sewerage, child malnutrition, and street conditions (with associated high accident rates).[38] Further, youth gangs were generally named separately, reflecting that in addition to their often criminal activities, the formation of youth gangs worries parents and shows that the social fabric of communities is threatened - be it for unemployment or other reasons.

The communities also discussed the causes of violence and possible solutions. For youth violence, the causes are perceived to be economic (youth unemployment) and the lack of supervision and a strong core of accepted behaviors and values. Proposed solutions are practical and restrained to what the community itself can do (possibly with some outside help): building sports facilities to lure the young off the streets, organizing training classes for parents, and conducting vocational training courses. With respect to domestic violence, all communities agreed that the major reason for family violence is a deterioration of respect among family members. Unanimously, the four communities that gave high priority to domestic violence suggested that mandatory classes be held for male household heads - such classes would discuss basic family values and the rights of women and children. Lastly, the communities agreed in large part on the causes of robberies and assaults: absent (or infrequent and irregular) police controls and too few neighborhood security committees. The communities consequently propose strengthening such security measures.

A violence survey (*Encuesta de Hogares sobre Violencia*, ENHOVI) was conducted by INEI to assess certain acts of violence in Lima in 1997. Using simple prediction models, we combined this violence survey with the ENAHO (1996) and were able to impute consumption levels for each household, which allowed us to look at the incidence of different types of violence by consumption decile.[39] Due to the sensitive nature of the topic, the survey excluded violence within the family, however.

We find that the overall incidence of violence is very high and that certain types of violence are linked to poverty level. Overall, more than one third of the population in Lima was victim to or witness of a violent act in 1997. As Graph 12 shows, robberies (in the street or house, or of the car) were more prevalent - as could be expected – among richer Lima residents but still significant for the poor. About 23 percent of the lowest four deciles were victims of or witnesses to such violence. The incidence of physical aggression was significantly

---

[38]   These rankings were obtained through general community meetings; specialized focus groups (e.g. by gender) could have resulted in different results but those were not conducted.

[39]   We imputed household consumption using the following procedure. First, we selected all variables which were in both the violence survey and the *Encuesta Nacional de Hogares* (1996). Second, we derived simple econometric models in which household consumption is a function of occupational status of household members, household size, access to services and education attainment of household members. Third, we used these models to impute household consumption. Finally, we derived consumption deciles by ranking households according to their per capita consumption level and using expansion factors supplied in the survey as weights.

lower than that for robbery but concentrated among the poor: the risk of being exposed to physical aggression in the poorest decile was about double the risk of that in the richest decile. The INEI survey (1997) reveals that in about half the cases of physical violence, the perpetrator was know to the victim. Finally, it is interesting to note that about 90 percent of all violent acts were not reported to the police, in one quarter of all cases because lack of trust in the authorities.

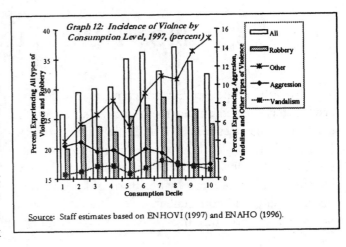

Source: Staff estimates based on ENHOVI (1997) and ENAHO (1996).

Mirroring the ranking exercise of the neighborhood communities in Ate, less than 10 percent of the poor felt safe in their neighborhood. Graph 13 depicts the percentage of the population in Lima who stated that they feel secure in their neighborhood. The security feeling is clearly linked to poverty levels, with about four times more Limenios in the richest decile feeling secure than in the poorest decile. This high insecurity feeling of the extreme poor limits their mobility and, with that, both their social interactions and earning possibilities.

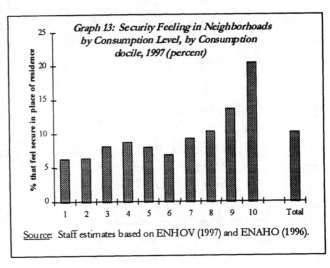

Source: Staff estimates based on ENHOV (1997) and ENAHO (1996).

31

5. GROWTH AND EMPLOYMENT

One of the biggest concerns in the Peruvian public debate on poverty is whether growth has created employment and whether this has led to poverty reduction. This section examines this question. It finds that, yes, growth over the past years has indeed created employment; about 1.3 million more people were in remunerated employment in 1997 compared to 1994. Many of these new jobs are informal so workers do not have signed contracts or are covered by health or old-age insurance. Also, productivity does not seem to be increasing and consequently, real wages are flat at best. The major impact of growth on poverty reduction has thus been through employment creation and not through real wage increases.

The section starts with general labor market trends and then analyzes the links among growth, poverty, and employment. We then present a number of different simulations of future poverty reduction possibilities, taking into account both possible varying regional and sectoral growth patterns.

LABOR MARKET TRENDS

In the years since 1994, 1.3 million new jobs were created in Peru. People finding jobs were a very small percentage of the unemployed but many more were newcomers to the labor market. The participation rate in Peru, already on the rise since the beginning of the decade, has again strongly increased. Table 19 shows that participation rates for men increased by 2.3 percent and for women by almost 7 percent between 1994 and 1997.

Table 19: Labor Force Participation Rates, 1994 and 1997

	male		female	
	1994	1997	1994	1997
Urban	75.6	79.9	45.2	53.1
Rural	91.4	91.3	64.9	72.9
Total	80.7	83.0	51.2	59.0

Source: Staff estimates based on ENNIV (1994,1997).

New jobs were created mainly in the informal urban sector of the economy. Using a legalistic definition of formality,[40] the increase in formal sector employment was slightly less than half a million while informal employment grew by more than 800,000 (Table 20). However, the term informality generally refers to the urban sector only since rural employment -

Table 20: Remunerated Job Creation, by Formal and Informal Sector, 1994-1997 ('000)

	formal	informal	TOTAL
Urban	430	585	1015
Rural	45	235	280
Total	475	820	1295

Source: Staff estimates based on ENNIV, (1994,1997).

---

[40] The legalistic definition defines the formal labor market as comprising all wage earners or the self-employed who pay taxes, are insured with the social security institute IPSS, have a signed contract, have rights to vacation, or belong to a union. See Saavedra and Chong (1999).

small-scale agriculture - is by its very nature informal. But even for the urban sector alone , the majority of jobs were created in informal employment, and that share of the informal sector increased slightly since 1994. As pointed out above, informality should not be equated with bad jobs as such activities can offer many of the poor a route out of poverty.

GROWTH PATTERN, POVERTY REDUCTION, AND SECTOR EMPLOYMENT GROWTH

Our analysis finds that employment growth was closely linked to poverty reduction. Table 21 looks at severe poverty rates and employment growth for the different sectors in the Peruvian economy.[41] As can be seen, the three sectors with the highest employment growth rates (construction, trade and commerce, and services) are also the three sectors that achieved the highest percentage decrease in poverty. Much of this employment growth provided families with more hours of work or a second source of income. Similarly, agriculture and mining/manufacturing had the lowest employment growth rates and also showed the lowest percentage reduction in the severe poverty rate.

Sector growth rates and employment creation are connected. As Table 21 reports

Table 21: Poverty Reduction by Sector and Growth Rates, 1994-1997					
Sectors	Severe Poverty Rate 1994 1997	perc. Change Sev. Pov. Rate 1994-1997	Employment Growth 1994-1997	Real GDP Growth (formal sector) 1994-1997	Distribution of Severe Poor 1997
	(1) (2)	(3)	(4)	(5)	(6)
Agriculture & forestry	31.8 26.4	-17.0	10.3	23.4	(30.4)
Construction	25.2 17.4	-31.0	63.9	33.8	(7.2)
Transport & communications	11.8 10.2	-13.0	18.0	n.a.	(7.8)
Trade and commerce	13.8 8.6	-37.5	43.9	22.8	(18.4)
Mining, petrol & manufacturing	9.2 8.4	- 8.5	7.9	13.7	(12.7)
Services	11.9 8.8	-26.0	21.6	8.4	(23.5)
TOTAL COUNTRY	18.8 14.8	-21.0	19.0	18.1	100

Source: Staff estimates based on ENNIV (1997). All households have been assigned a primary sector, e.g., the sector of the main income earner. Real GDP growth rates from Central Bank of Peru (1998).

(column 4), the push sectors in Peru over the last years were agriculture, construction, and trade. However, these real growth rates capture only the output of formal enterprises and do not necessarily account for many informal economic activities; thus, strictly speaking, the growth and employment data cannot be directly compared. Nevertheless, the two can be thought of as closely linked - if formal sector growth is high in a specific sector, supporting or

---

[41] To link sectors of the economy and poverty, we assign a household to a sector based on the primary occupation of the household head. This leaves only about 80 households unaccounted for (non-active household heads), and we neglect these in the table and calculations.

parallel informal enterprises should also realize an upswing. On face value, Peru's growth pattern was pro-poor over the time period because it was driven by the sectors in which severe poverty rates were highest (columns 1 and 2).

In construction and trade real growth translated into employment growth and poverty reduction. But one of the key factors explaining inequality and poverty developments over the past years in Peru is that the impressive agricultural growth rates did not translate fully into employment creation. Real growth rates in that sector are estimated at 23 percent over the 1994-1997 period (column 5 in Table 21); after construction, agriculture is the best performing sector. Growth has especially been strong in non-traditional exports. Agricultural productivity was seriously depressed at the beginning of the 1990s, so one can expect growth to be generated in large part by the existing work force working longer hours. This would be one possible explanation for the relatively low growth elasticity of employment generation in agriculture. This explains, to a large extent, the growing regional urban-rural inequality in Peru as well as slower social progress in rural Peru.

GROWTH AND POVERTY REDUCTION: SIMULATIONS

A number of simulations show how important continued growth is for poverty reduction but also how unequal, anti-poor growth can reduce or eradicate the potential benefits of economic expansion.

Growth will remain the backbone of any successful poverty reduction strategy in Peru. The simulations we employed were very simple and distributed the gains from growth (higher income and consumption) in society using the household survey from 1997 as the basic tool.[42] For example, the simulations do not take into account that productivity developments and hence the link between growth and employment creation will vary by sector. Further, we also abstract from mobility across sectors. The simulations do show, however, that the pattern and distribution of income gains matter for poverty reduction.

Graph 14 shows that Peru could reduce severe poverty by a further 25 percent in the coming five years if it were to achieve a real per capita growth rate of 3 percent. Higher growth rates would mean faster percent reduction of severe poverty - a 7 percent real per capita growth rate would reduce severe poverty by half in five years. However, as we have seen from 1994 to 1997, inequality cannot be assumed to be constant. If the trend of increasing inequality were to continue and

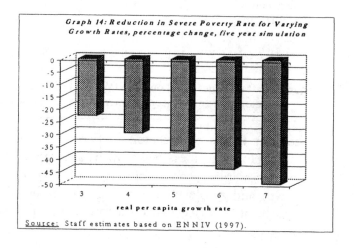

Graph 14: Reduction in Severe Poverty Rate for Varying Growth Rates, percentage change, five year simulation

real per capita growth rate

Source: Staff estimates based on ENNIV (1997).

---

[42] This assumes that incomes (and consumption) are related to the overall growth rate in the economy through productivity (and wage) increases or through the creation of new employment for secondary work or additional income earners.

the society were to become considerably more unequal, growth might not translate into poverty reduction at all: if the richest 20 percent of the population increase their consumption by 10 percent while the economy grows at 3 percent, the rich would simply reap all the benefits from growth. Severe poverty would not fall. In the reverse case, if inequality falls and the poorest 40 percent of the population increases its share of total consumption from 20 to 25 percent, severe poverty could be reduced by more than 60 percent.

Table 22: Simulation of Severe Poverty Reduction: Different Assumption About Inequality (real growth rate of 3 percent for 5 years)	
Simulation	Severe Poverty Reduction (percent)
Inequality constant	-23.0
Inequality increase[1]	0
Inequality decrease[2]	-62.0

Source: Staff estimates based on ENNIV (1997).
1   an increase in inequality implies that the richest 20 percent of the population in crease their share of total consumption from 43 to 50 percent.
2   a decrease in inequality means here that the poorest 40 percent of the population increase their share of total consumption from 20 to 25 percent.

The pattern of growth matters for poverty reduction. Again, these simulations are highly stylized as they assume that sector growth translates directly into growth of household consumption via additional employment and real wage changes (and we saw above that for the agricultural sector this relationship did not hold from 1994 to 1997). Further, these simulations assume no feedback effects - for example, that growth in export sectors would lead to technological spillovers, as is generally found. However, the simulations do provide an interesting comparison of how different patterns of growth matter for the

Table 23: Simulation of Severe Poverty Reduction: Different Sectoral Growth Rates (real growth rate of 3 percent for five years)		
Simulation	Sectors	Severe Poverty Reduction
Growth of high-poverty sectors	agriculture, construction	-49.2
Growth of medium-poverty sectors	mining, petroleum, manufacturing, trade transport, commun.	-27.7
Growth of low-poverty sectors	services	-24.3

Source: Staff Estimates based on ENNIV 1997. The simulations assume that the growth rate of high growth sectors is 6 percent with all other sectors growing equally at the residual growth rate.

poor. Table 23 recaps the findings. We find that if growth is pro-poor, that is, concentrated in agriculture and construction, severe poverty would be reduced by more than half in five years with an overall annual per capita growth in all sectors of 3 percent. On the other hand, if growth were to be concentrated in services, the impact on severe poverty would be only 25 percent. While growth should not be artificially tilted towards the pro-poor sectors, investment in these sectors will depend on a continuation of policies that do not discriminate against them.

Closely linked to this strong impact of the sector growth is the impact of different regional patterns of development. Severe poverty reduction would be strongest if the rural sectors (with all on-farm agricultural and off-farm activities) were to carry Peruvian economic progress in the coming years. Table 24 shows the results for this

Table 24: Simulation of Severe Poverty Reduction: Different Regional Growth Rates (real growth rate of 3 percent for five years)	
Simulation	Severe Poverty Reduction
Lima	-22.3
Other urban areas	-26.4
Rural areas	-47.0

Source: Staff estimates based on ENNIV (1997). The simulations assume that the growth rate of high growth region is 6 percent with all other regions growing equally at 3 percent.

calculation. The severe poverty decline would be similar to the one observed with agriculture and construction growth: almost 50 percent. If Lima were to continue its role as the engine of growth, however, severe poverty reduction could be much smaller - around a 22 percent decline.

THE TASK AHEAD: RAISING PRODUCTIVITY AND REAL INCOMES.

One of the major tasks in the coming years is to raise productivity and, with it, real incomes. Until now, employment generation has not been accompanied by real income increases (Graphs 15 and 16). For Lima, graphs 15 and 16 show real income developments in both the formal and informal sectors since 1986. As can be seen, hyperinflation contracted real wage income enormously in 1990 and the recovery period of the economy went hand in hand with increasing real wages. However, with very few exceptions, real incomes have remained flat since 1991 and in some sectors even show declining trends. These trends are matched very closely by overall productivity developments in the country.[43] In terms of levels, real wages remain - independent of sector and type of occupation - below their level of 12 years ago. The

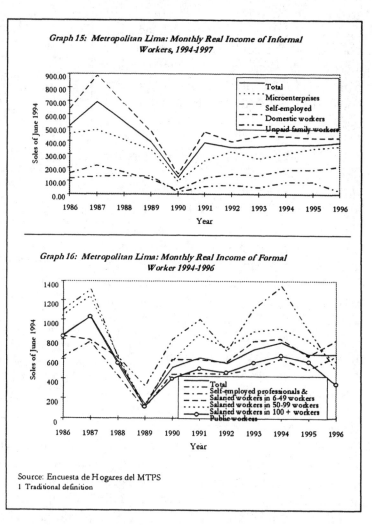

Graph 15: Metropolitan Lima: Monthly Real Income of Informal Workers, 1994-1997

Graph 16: Metropolitan Lima: Monthly Real Income of Formal Worker 1994-1996

Source: Encuesta de Hogares del MTPS
1 Traditional definition

Peruvian experience of real income and productivity developments is not atypical for countries having undergone structural reforms. In Brazil, wages increased only slightly since the liberalization in 1991. In Chile, real wages were basically stagnant for about 10 years after the recession of 1982 and the market-oriented reforms. Rising labor force participation increases labor supply and dampens wage increases. Nevertheless, the more the government supports the private sector to raise productivity, the quicker will real income changes filter through the economy: supporting public infrastructure investment, training support, and education of the next generation of wage-earners can all contribute to this.

---

[43]   Saavedra (1998).

6. SOCIAL EXPENDITURES - WHAT AND FOR WHOM?

To complement the analysis of poverty comparisons, we have one major question still to answer: what was the role of public programs in poverty reduction? Did they help to reduce poverty? Or were they in the end of little value to the recipients? This section will present available material to answer this question - but we will fall short of establishing a clear link between public programs and poverty reduction. To shed light on this topic, we would need detailed information on households *before* and *after* an intervention, e.g. the well-being of a household before and after it receives nutritional aid through the Glass of Milk program. And we would need a control group, i.e., families that are similar in their characteristics but did not benefit from the same program. We had hoped that the panel data, containing information about identical households over time, would serve for this analysis, but unfortunately, we were not able to clearly establish which specific programs had what kind of effect on household welfare, partly because the sample size was severely limited. The only clear result we obtained, as reported earlier, concerned the provision of public services in water, sanitation, and electricity: these raised families' welfare and, in addition, had a bundling effect - three services having more than three times the effect of one service. However, since literally dozens of programs finance this type of infrastructure we could not distinguish which ones were successful and which ones were not.

What we can do in this section, though, are two things: first, take an aggregate view of social expenditures and anti-poverty programs, and assess whom they benefited and how many people they reached - without judging whether they were successful or not. For this analysis we used the *Encuesta Nacional de Hogares* (1996) from the Statistical Institute of Peru (INEI), a survey considerably larger (20,000 households) than that of the Instituto Cuánto. Second, we can analyze the short-term impact of direct transfer programs on poverty.

SOCIAL EXPENDITURES IN 1996

Before presenting our results on the distribution of aggregate social expenditures, one cautious remark needs to be made: figures presented here relate to the average incidence of program expenditures, i.e., what percentage reached which group in the population. Basing policy decisions on such an average incidence might be misleading as the distribution of marginal expenditures might be very different. Or in other words, a program might benefit largely the non-poor in society at a given point in time. However, the *additional* program budget might go directly to the poor, so a policy decision on the average performance might not be wise. Such a gap between the distribution of average and additional expenditures is likely to be high for programs that have a large part of their current budget linked to past investments (e.g. education or health programs). The difference will not be very pronounced for programs that finance short-maturation projects and then move on to different sites, as is common under the social investment funds.

Aggregate Distribution. We examine expenditures in the education and health sectors, in housing and infrastructure programs, and in a number of specialized anti-poverty programs.[44] Together, these programs accounted for a total expenditure of 7.6 billion soles, or roughly 40 percent of the *total* public budget. Of that, about 55 percent was in the education sector, 25 percent in health, 12 percent in housing, and basic infrastructure programs, and 8 percent in the anti-poverty programs.

Table 25: Budget Examined in Analysis (1996), billion soles	
Education	4.1
Health	1.9
Housing & Infrastructure	1.0
Anti-Poverty Programs	0.6
Total	7.6

Source: *Comision de Presupuesto del Congreso;* Saavedra (1998)

Looking at the general distribution of expenditures, the first observation is that, in 1996, they went mostly to the urban areas. We estimate that about 70 percent of the examined expenditure went to urban Peru and this is likely to be an underestimate, since we assume - as is common in incidence analyses - that the per capita benefit to beneficiaries is equal across the country. It is all too well known, however, that per beneficiary expenditures in health and education are much lower in rural areas (see Graph 11 above). Table 26 reports that only one program or line of activity targeted the majority of its expenditure to rural areas in 1996: the social fund FONCODES, which had formulated an explicit strategy to target the rural poor at the beginning of the year. It is likely that FONCODES increased its total budget allocation to rural areas in 1997 even further, given its targeting strategy. It is therefore a clear exception to the largely urban bias of other social programs.

Table 26: Rural/Urban Distribution of Government Expenditures, 1996		
	sector	share of exp. received by rural residents
Education & health sectors:		
Basic education	education	47
Secondary education	education	19
University education	education	6
Basic health	health	50
Hospital care	health	16
by programs:		
FONCODES	various	68
PRONAA	nutrition	44
INABIF	children	2
FONAVI	elec & water	20
ENACE	housing	10
BanMat	housing	11
INFES	education	16
Total		30
memo:		
Share of poor in rural (1997)		47
Share of severe poor in rural (1997)		58

Source: Staff estimates based on ENAHO (1996).

---

[44] The anti-poverty programs include FONCODES, PRONAA, COOPOP, INABIF and INFES. The housing and infrastructure programs include ENACE, BanMat and Ute-FONAVI.

Aggregate Social Expenditures Distribution. Examining the total budget of 7.6 billion soles considered here, expenditures were mildly tilted toward the better-off in society. Only about 17 percent of expenditures went to the poorest 20 percent (Table 27). It appears that if expenditure distribution was largely driven by the population distribution rather than by poverty level, this was already observed above when we looked at the distribution of total expenditures by urban and rural area - there, as well as by poverty group, we cannot (on such an aggregate level) detect the targeting of expenditures to the weakest in society. Given that the budget we look at here is the social and anti-poverty budget, this is a disappointing result.

Table 27: Aggregate Distribution of Social Expenditures	
quintile	*share of total expenditure*
1 (poorest)	16.6
2	18.6
3	21.2
4	22.4
5 (wealthiest)	21.1

Source: Staff Estimates based on ENAHO (1996).

Education and Health Expenditure Distribution. As observed in many countries, Peruvian expenditures in basic education and basic health were progressive in 1996, while most higher-level spending went to the better-off in society. Graphs 17 and 18 present education and health Lorenz curves for 1996 with the horizontal axis representing the population distribution and the vertical axis the distribution of expenditures. As can be seen primary education expenditures were considerably more progressive than secondary and higher education expenditures. For the higher education expenditures, about half of total expenditures supported the richest 20 percent in society. Similarly, hospital care (both ambulatory and stationary) was considerably more regressive than primary health care - 30 percent of resources went to the top population quintile.

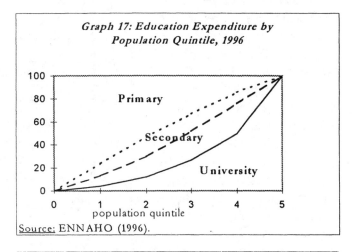

Graph 17: Education Expenditure by Population Quintile, 1996

Source: ENNAHO (1996).

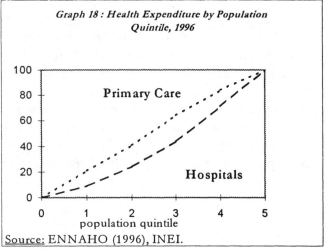

Graph 18 : Health Expenditure by Population Quintile, 1996

Source: ENNAHO (1996), INEI.

39

Coverage and Targeting Rates. While education and health programs, by their very nature are (or should be) universal programs, the other programs and projects looked at here intend to reach specific groups in society. FONCODES, for example, aimed at reaching the extreme poor in the rural areas in 1996, and PRONAA wanted to reach poor families with malnourished children.

To assess how well these programs did in 1996, we want to measure their success using two indicators. The first is the coverage rate. This is simply the percentage of the poor population reached. The second is the targeting performance, i.e., the percentage of total expenditures that actually went to the intended beneficiaries and did not escape to better-off groups. It should be noted, though, that several of the programs considered here, especially the housing and basic infrastructure programs, did not have the articulated aim of reaching the poor in society. Nevertheless, we want to hold them to the above criteria.

We find that FONCODES and PRONAA have the best record in reaching their beneficiaries and targeting their expenditures. Graph 19 shows both of these indicators together. Against the horizontal axis we plot the coverage rate, i.e., the percentage of the poorest 40 percent reached. Against the horizontal axis we measure the concentration of expenditures in the same two quintiles - our targeting indicator. A program that reaches a substantial

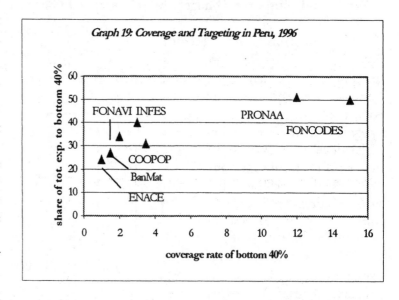

Graph 19: Coverage and Targeting in Peru, 1996

portion of the population (i.e., has a high coverage rate) and at the same time manages to concentrate its resources in the poorest two quintiles would get an entry in the upper right corner. On the other hand, programs that reach few of the poor and concentrate only a small percentage of their total resources on them would end up in the lower left-hand corner. As can be seen in the graph, coverage rates for most programs were relatively small - mostly below 5 percent. And concentration shares were also relatively low; most programs spent less than 40 percent in the bottom two quintiles. The social fund FONCODES and PRONAA were exceptions - both of them show a progressive distribution of expenditures and a relatively large coverage rate (see Box 2 for an evaluation of nutrition programs).

Box 2: Nutrition Programs in Peru -- Targeting Rates, Coverage Rates, and Benefit Distribution

Coverage rates of the nutritional programs are, by international standards, very high. In 1997, about 60 percent of poor households received some nutritional benefit from one of the many nutritional programs. The biggest of these programs are the Glass of Milk program (*Vaso de Leche*, Ministry of Finance, working through municipalities), the School Breakfast Program (administered by FONCODES), and the local soup kitchens *(Comedores Populares*, financed largely by PRONAA). The adjacent table breaks the households in the population into four different groups by poverty and malnutrition levels (households with at least one malnourished child fall in the malnourished category). Results show relatively good targeting and high coverage rates of nutrition programs *evaluated jointly*, with the poor households with at least one malnourished infant showing a coverage rate of 66 percent. The non-poor households with well-fed infants show a much lower coverage rate, of 23.7 percent. However, the progressiveness of this transfer is considerably smaller if we calculate the net monetary transfer equivalent (taking into account frequency and quantity of the transfer). Taken together, leakage of the nutritional programs (i.e., transfers neither to the poor nor the households with malnourished children) is about 24 percent. On a regional basis, the rural Sierra receives considerably less in transfers in 1997 than it should given that about 51 percent of all malnourished children live there. Lima receives a much larger share than it would were expenditures distributed in accordance with the geographical prevalence of malnutrition.

Malnutrition Programs: Distribution of Real Program Benefits, 1997

group	coverage	monetary benefit
malnutr.& poor	66.3	38.0
malnour. & non-poor	43.3	22.3
non-malnuri & poor	47.0	15.9
non-malnur. & non-poor	23.7	23.8
		(100)

Source: Staff Estimates based on ENNIV (1997).

Distribution of malnourished children and distribution of nutrition transfers, 1997

	distribution of the malnourished	distribution of program exp.
Lima	8.9	31.6
Urb. Coast	6.9	8.8
Rur. Coast	5.1	9.6
Urb. Sierra	7.7	5.3
Rur. Sierra	51.3	31.9
Urb. Jungle	5.1	4.4
Rural Jungle	15.0	8.4
	(100)	(100)

Source: Staff Estimates based on ENNIV (1997).

As can be seen from the coverage rates, Peru's nutrition programs are very large. According to the Budget Commission, spending on the nutritional programs of PRONAA, the Glass of Milk program, of the Ministry of Education, and FONCODES alone increased from US$ 190 million in 1994 to about US$ 250 million in 1997. But there are many more programs, administered centrally and by municipalities; for example, *PACFO (Programa de Complementacion Alimentaria para Grupos en Mayor Riesgo;* Supplementary Feeding Program for High Risk Groups) in the Ministry of Health which targets the 5 poorest departments in the central Sierra. One of the biggest problems in the sector is that the Ministry of Women and Human Development is formally responsible for diagnosing the nutrition situation and establishing nutrition policies, program objectives, implementation norms, and standards. But the Ministry has only very limited authority over many policies and programs, some of which have no nutritional objectives per se but are rather geared toward income generation or school attendance.

Reasons for Poor Program Targeting. Many studies have analyzed the quite meager coverage and targeting performance of the social programs described in this section. The reasons found are: (a) little use of (existing) poverty maps (except for FONCODES and PRONAA); (b) an urban tilt in expenditure distribution, which means that many of the extremely poor in rural areas cannot be reached; and (c) criteria for program access which exclude many of the poor (especially in the housing credit programs ENACE and Banmat). For both nutrition programs and programs of selected ministries, such as the Ministry of the Presidency, it has been repeatedly observed that many programs overlap in functions, are not centrally coordinated and are subject to arbitrary expenditure decisions.[45] Targeting maps, if used, have been found useful for expenditure allocation. However, the map most widely used by FONCODES was found to contain a serious error. The map is based on the construction of a poverty index which is itself an aggregate of several indicators. As a consequence of the aggregation procedure, malnutrition which was supposed to have the highest weight in the poverty index was assigned a much lower importance - 15 percent instead of 50 percent whereas the roof type of houses was weighted with 40 percent instead of the planned 7 percent (World Bank, 1996). Similarly, recent analytical work also questions the poverty map now used by the Ministry of the Presidency in its *Lucha Contra la Pobreza* (Fight Against Poverty Program).[46] Because this map uses the number of the poor per district as one of the key variables determining expenditure allocation instead of the poverty rate or poverty depth, it heavily tilts resources to larger districts in urban areas. In fact, the per capita expenditure distribution under this scheme is found to be worse than if resources were allocated on a purely population basis.

POVERTY IMPACT OF DIRECT TRANSFERS

Unlike the basic and social services programs, direct transfer programs are geared to help poor families in the short run. In Peru, these programs comprise mainly the many large nutritional programs, but also include the employment programs, e.g. of FONCODES. Further, we can also count pension payments from the National Security Institute as a public transfer. How important are these public transfers for families? And how important are these public transfers compared to private transfers from friends, neighbors, and family members?

We analyze the effect of transfers by estimating the impact they have on poverty rates. In reality, transfers might not increase household welfare in the short run for all families. For example, if food donations replace the purchase of food, family income might be saved, used to repay credit, or spent in a way that is not beneficial to the poorest in the family. However, this exercise assumes that all transfers received have been used in their full amount to increase household consumption. Since we want to compare public with private transfers, we make the same assumption for family aid, private pensions, and remittances from home or abroad. Public transfers here do not include education and health expenditures or basic and productive service investments.

---

[45]   See, for example, Homedes (1996) and World Bank (1996)

[46]   See Schady (1998).

42

We find that total public transfers have hypothetically a much lower impact on poverty than private transfers. Table 28 examines the impact of a number of different transfers on poverty and extreme poverty. By far the most important transfer for the poor and extremely poor alike are not public transfers but private national transfers followed by private pensions and employer benefits. Food aid is the most important public transfer and has a quite significant impact on severe poverty in the rural areas but is less significant in urban areas.

Table 28: Impact of Private and Public Transfers on Poverty and Severe Poverty, 1997
(Percentage Impact on Poverty Rate from Different Types of Transfers)

	poverty rate		severe poverty rate	
	urban	rural	urban	rural
food aid	-1.2	-1.7	-0.9	-3.0
other public transfers	-0.3	-0.3	-0.1	-0.5
public pension	-0.1	-0.1	-0.2	-0.1
private pension or employer benefit	-4.6	-1.3	-3.5	-1.3
private transfers, national	-4.3	-2.7	-3.5	-3.5
private transfers, international	-1.1	-0.1	-0.8	-0.1
all public combined	-1.4	-2.4	-1.2	-3.6
all private combined	-9.6	-3.9	-8.2	-5.1

Source: Staff estimates based on ENNIV (1997).

7. INSTITUTIONS - FROM INDIVIDUAL SECTOR STRATEGIES TO A CONSISTENT AND BROAD-BASED ANTI-POVERTY FOCUS

This report does not provide detailed recommendations as to how Peru can make further and effective inroads against poverty. Such specific policy recommendations have been and will be made by specialized studies. The purpose of this report has been to take a more global, aggregate view of social progress over the years 1994 through 1997, based on largely evidence of the distribution of public investment and social programs. This section, therefore, takes a look at social policy formulation in Peru at a more macro level.

Current Social Policy Formulation. Today, the multitude of social policy programs operate largely independently, try to reach their beneficiaries through different means, and lack stringent evaluation. Expenditures of many of these programs, although well intentioned, are often isolated in nature, and do not reach the poorest in society. The Ministry of the Presidency alone has six programs in the education sector - in addition to all of those of the Ministry of Education. The many nutrition programs are administered by the ministries of Finance (*Vaso de Leche*), Women and Human Development (PRONAA), Health (Basic Health Project, PACFO), Education and the Ministry of the Presidency (FONCODES). The Inter-ministerial Council on Social Affairs (CIAS) has the responsibility to ensure smooth inter-ministerial information flow and guide social policy development. Recently, CIAS has assumed a more active role in setting technical standards and offering technical assistance to line ministries. It still operates without clear mandate and resources, however.

Conflicting Decrees. The need for the empowerment of one central social policy unit becomes quite apparent if we look at two important recent presidential decrees. The first decree (012-97-PCM of April 1, 1997) makes the Presidency of the Council of Ministers, and with it the social policy coordination council (CIAS), responsible for coordinating and improving the allocation of social expenditures among agencies and ministries. The second decree (030-97-PCM of June 20 1997) officially adopted the targeting and coordination strategy of the *Lucha Contra La Pobreza*, which was developed and is managed by the Ministry of the Presidency. The decree called for the widespread application of the strategy by the whole public sector, making - de facto - the Ministry of the Presidency responsible for social policy coordination.

Institutions Matter. We believe that one of the most pressing needs in the fight against poverty in Peru is institutional reform, which is a precondition for achieving a much bigger impact with available funds. A recent study of Latin American countries, *Beyond the Washington Consensus: Institutions Matter*[47], shows that the quality of institutions have a significant positive influence on both economic growth and poverty reduction. The study described the decision-

---

[47] Burki and Perry (1997).

making process in Peru as *informal*, i.e., the *de jure* system is in reality mostly ovetaken by a very different *de facto*, or informal, system. One of the key characteristics of such an informal system is a parallel organizational structure in Peru (especially of key autonomous agencies), substantially by-passing the cabinet and ministerial structure.

We believe that one of the most pressing needs in the fight against poverty in Peru is institutional reform, which is a precondition for achieving a much bigger impact with available funds. First, economic and social policymaking would need to be more closely integrated, informed by sound technical analysis and advice. Many different poverty maps and targeting mechanisms currently employed need to be harmonized, since poverty is reduced most effectively if interventions are provided jointly and in a coordinated manner. In Peru, conflicting decrees empowering the Ministry of the Presidency and CIAS currently exist, but neither of the institutions has true power or manpower.

Box 3: Multi-Sector Social Policy Formulation in Brazil: The Comunidade Solidaria

Brazil's *Comunidade Solidaria* (CS) constitutes a direct link between Government and society. Its task is to identify and address cross-sector social problems outside the sphere of the Federal Government but linked to its policymaking and program mechanisms. The Consultative Council of CS is comprised of 11 ministries, the Executive Secretariat of the CS, and 21 representatives from civil society including business, NGOs, and voluntary organizations. Its aim is to mobilize social efforts, implement innovative projects at local levels, and identify social priorities. The Executive Secretariat of the CS is linked to the Civil Affairs Office of the President of the Republic, with representatives from sector ministries, provinces and municipalities, and civil society. Consultations between local organizations and municipal and federal governments have led to the formulation of a Basic Agenda, which constitutes an action plan for local anti-poverty programs.

Funds provided to Basic Agenda social programs are in the form of periodic transfers from ministries and federal bodies to state and municipal governments. Transfers have grown from R$980 million in 1995 to R$2.5 billion in 1997, and are predicted to increase to R$2.9 billion in 1998. Most funds are designated for the poorest regions in Brazil across social sectors. The total number of municipalities participating has also increased significantly, from 302 in 1995 to 1,368 in 1997.

Closely linked to the above, pro-poor policies require good targeting and thorough evaluation. Many different poverty maps and targeting mechanisms are currently used in Peru and these can be harmonized. However, program planning and monitoring go beyond the need for targeting and prioritization. They involve policymakers being able to assess whether a certain intervention did indeed help or not. And it also implies that policymakers and technicians are able to assess how *changes* in program nature and how *changes* in expenditures are distributed and what effect they have.

Third, central coordination can go hand in hand with decentralized execution that includes other partners in the fight against poverty. Examples from other Latin American countries show that private-voluntary-public partnerships in poverty reduction at the local level can be extremely successful (Box 3).[48] One reason such partnerships are successful

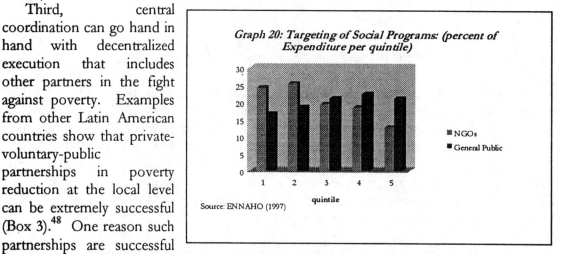

Graph 20: Targeting of Social Programs: (percent of Expenditure per quintile)

Source: ENNAHO (1997)

is that each organization brings its comparative advantage to the table: central government brings financing and organization; municipal government brings administrative and local knowledge; NGOs and community-based organizations offer direct understanding of (and link to) problems of the poor. INEI's *Encuesta Nacional de Hogares* (1996) shows that NGO-administered programs have a significantly better targeting record than most of the public programs and match the targeting results of programs administered by FONCODES and PRONAA (Graph 20).

---

[48] Fiszbein and Lowden (1998) have collected a large number of examples of how government, business and civic partnerships have worked successfully for poverty reduction in Latin America.

REFERENCES

Altamirano, Teofilo (1988), Cultura Andina y Pobreza Urbana, Pontifica Universidad Catolica del Peru, Lima.

Burki, Shahid and Guillermo Perry (1997), Beyond the Washington Consensus: Institutions Matter, World Bank Latin American and Caribbean Studies, Washington D.C.

CARITAS (1997), La Extrema Pobreza en el Area Rural en Peru, Lima.

Central Bank of Peru (1998), Boletin Mensual, Lima.

Davis, Shelton and Harry Patroninos (1996), Investing in Latin America's Indigenous peoples: The Human and Social Capital Dimensions, Seminar on Indigenous Peoples Production and Trade, Copenhagen, Denmark, 15-17 January 1996.

Deaton, Angus (1997), The Analysis of Household Surveys, Johns Hopkins University Press for the World Bank, Baltimore.

Deininger, Klaus and Lyn Squire (1996), A New Data Set Measuring Income Inequality, World Bank Economic Review 10, pp. 565-591.

Escobal, Javier, Jaime Saavedra and Maximo Torero (1998), Los Activos de los Pobres en el Peru, Documentos del Trabajo, Lima, Grupo de Análisis para el Desarrollo.

Fallon, Peter (1998), Dispersion of Sub-National Regional Income per Capita, World Bank website, Sub-National Economic Policy, World Bank.

Ferreira, Francisco and Julie Litchfield (1998), Calm after the Storms: Income Distribution in Chile, 1987-1994, World Bank Working Paper 1960, Washington D.C.

Fiszbein, Ariel and Pamela Lowden (1998), Working Together for a Change: Government, Business and Civic Partnerships for Poverty Reduction in Latin America, Economic Development Institute, World Bank.

Francke, Pedro (1997), Realmente Ha Aumentado la Pobreza en los Ultimos Dos Años?, mimeo, Banco Central de Reserva, Lima.

Glewwe, Paul and Gillete Hall (1995), Who is Most Vulnerable to Macroeconomic Shocks? Hypotheses Tests Using Panel Data from Peru, Living Standard Measurement Study 117, World Bank.

Hentschel, Jesko and Peter Lanjouw (1996), Constructing an Indicator of Consumption for the Analysis of Poverty, Living Standard Measurement Discussion Paper Series 124, World Bank, Washington D.C.

Hicks, Norman and Pia Peeters (1998), Social Indicators and Per Capita Income in Latin America, processed, Latin America and Caribbean Regional Office, World Bank, Washington D.C.

Homedes, Nuria (1996), Nutrition Note, Latin America and Caribbean Regional Office, processed, World Bank.

Instituto Cuánto (1997), Mil Quinientas Familias Dos Años Despues: La Pobreza en el Peru, 1994-1996, Lima.

Instituto Nacional de Estadística e Informática (1996), Encuesta Nacional de Hogares, Lima.

Instituto Nacional de Estadística e Informática (1997), Encuesta de Hogares Sobre Victimizacion, Lima.

International Monetary Fund(1998), Peru – Selected Issues, Western Hemisphere Department, Washington.

Lanjouw, Jean Olson (1997), Behind the Line, mimeo, United Nations Development Program, New York.

Lanjouw, Jean Olson and Peter Lanjouw (1997), Poverty Comparisons with Non-Comparable Data, Policy Research Working Paper 1709, World Bank.

Lanjouw, Peter (1998), Ecuador's Rural Nonfarm Sector as a Route out of Poverty, Policy Research Working Paper Series 1904, World Bank.

Lanjouw, Peter, Giovanna Prennushi and Salman Zaidi (1996), Building Blocks of a Consumption-Based Analysis of Poverty in Nepal, mimeo, Development Economics Research Group, World Bank.

Lanjouw, Peter and Martin Ravallion (1995), Poverty and Household Size, Economic Journal, Vol. 105, No. 433.

Londoño, Juan Luis and Miguel Székely (1997), Distributional Surprises After a Decade of Reforms: Latin America in the Nineties, Inter-American Development Bank, Washington D.C.

Lopez, Ramon and Carla della Maggiora (1998), Rural Poverty in Peru: Stylized Facts and Analytics for Policy, processed, University of Maryland, College Park.

Luerssen, Susan (1993), Illness and Household Reproduction in a Highly Monetized Rural Economy: A Case from the Southern Peruvian Highlands, Journal of Anthropological Research 49, pp.255-281.

MacIsaac, Donna and Jesko Hentschel (1996), Poverty and Inequality in Urban Poverty, in: Ecuador Poverty Report, World Bank, Washington D.C.

MacIsaac, Donna and Harry Patrinos (1995), Labour Market Discrimination against Indigenous People in Peru, Journal of Development Studies, Vol. 32, pp. 218-233.

Ministry of the Presidency (1997), Plan de Accion Local en Ate, Lima.

Moncada, Gilberto and Richard Webb (1996), Como Estamos? Analisis de la Encuesta de Niveles de Vida, Insituto Cuánto, Lima.

Moncada, Gilberto (1996), Perfil de la Pobreza en Peru, 1994, in Webb, Richard and Gilberto Moncada, Como Estamos?, Instituto Cuánto, Lima, pp. 97-135.

Moser, Caroline (1996), Urban Poverty: How do Households Adjust?, in: Ecuador Poverty Report, World Bank.

Oxford Analytica (1998), Peru: Poverty Programs, The Fujimori Government's Strategy to Tackle Rural Poverty, July 30.

Persaud, Thakoor (1992), Housing Delivery Systems and the Urban Poor, A Comparison Among Six Latin Countries, Latin America and the Caribbean Regional Studies Program 23, Washington D.C.

Ravallion, Martin (1994), Poverty Comparisons, Harwood Academic Publishers, Chur.

Rodriguez, Edgard (1998), Toward a More Equal Income Distribution? The Case of Peru 1994-97, background report for this study, processed, Poverty Reduction and Economic Management Network, Poverty Group, World Bank.

Rodriguez, José and David Abler (1998), Asistencia a la Escuela y Participacíon en el Mercado Laboral de los Menores en el Peru entre 1985 y 1994, processed, Pennsylvania State University.

Saavedra, Jaime (1998), What Do We Know About Poverty and Income Distribution in Peru with Emphasis on Its Links with Education and the Labor Market, background report for this study, Grupo de Análisis para el Desarrollo, Lima.

Saavedra, Jaime and Alberto Chong (1999), Structural Reform, Institutions, and Earnings: Evidence from the Formal and Informal Sectors in Urban Peru, Journal of Development Studies, forthcoming.

Saavedra, Jaime and Juan Jose Diaz (1997), El Rol del Capital Humano en la Distribucion del Ingreso, mimeo, Grupo de Análisis para el Desarrollo, Lima.

Saavedra, Jaime, R. Melzi and A. Miranda (1997), Financiamiento de la Educacion, Documento de Trabajo 24, Grupo de Análisis para el Desarrollo, Lima.

Schady, Norbert (1998), Picking the Poor: Indicators of Geographical Targeting in Peru, Woodrow Wilson School of Government, Princeton University, processed, Princeton.

United Nations (1997a), Human Development Report, New York.

United Nations (1997b), Informe Sobre el Desarrollo Humano del Peru, Lima.

White, Michael J., Lorenzo Moreno and Shenyang Gua (1995), The Interrelation of Fertility and Geographic Mobility in Peru: a Hazards Model Analysis, International Migration Review 29, pp. 492-514.

World Bank (1996), Did the Ministry of the Presidency Reach the Poor in 1995?, processed, Country Department 6, Latin America and the Caribbean Region, World Bank.

World Bank (1998), World Development Indicators, Washington D.C.

Yamada, Gustavo (1996), Urban Informal Employment and Self-Employment in Developing Countries: Theory and Evidence, Economic Development and Cultural Change 44, 289-314.

ANNEX I: PANEL STUDY OF HOUSEHOLDS

This annex briefly recaps the results of studying the panel subsample of the Living Standard Measurement Surveys for which the same households were interviewed in 1994 and again in 1997.

Our basic model consisted of expressing the growth of per capita household expenditures from 1994 to 1997 as a function of a large number of exogenous variables, such as access to basic services, initial education and consumption level, etc. Many of these variables are household characteristics in the initial year (1994). They include years of the household head, education of the household head, migration, language spoken etc.

Since many of the households changed in size or headship over the three years, we looked at three different, increasingly restrictive panel subsamples to test the robustness of the estimates. The first sample includes the total panel of 891 households (*full sample*) . The second sample included only those households that had the same headship in 1994 and 1997 (690 households). The third and most restrictive sample included only those households that neither changed in headship nor composition over the years – for this sub-sample, per capita growth in household consumption is not influenced by additions or attrition from the household.

Our first result confirms other panel analyses in Peru: mobility in the sample is very high, i.e. a large percentage of households changed their relative position by more than one welfare decile over the three years (see Glewwe and Hall 1995, Escobal et al 1998). In absolute terms, about 55 percent of all households recorded a per capita consumption growth of more than 10 percent, about 15 percent recorded more or less the same consumption level and 30 percent had a consumption per capita level in 1997 more than 10 percent below their level in 1994.[49]

Regressions results using the three samples are similar. The regression result for the full panel is reproduced in table A1.1. Robust results from the regressions, which hold for a variety of different specifications and application to the different sub-samples, are:

a.   *Female-headed households.* Controlling for all other influences (education, initial consumption, household size, dependency ratio etc.) female-headed households fared better than male ones, increasing per capita consumption growth by 0.11 percent (in the full panel).

b.   *Migrant families.* We do not find evidence that migrant households (i.e., the household head was born in a different location than he/she lived in 1994) fared worse than non-migrant families. The parameter is positive and insignificant in the full sample and becomes marginally significant and positive in the most restricted sample.

---

[49]   In part, the high mobility could be due to measurement errors. This can cause serious econometric problems for difference or growth regressions (see Deaton 1997, pp.108-110).

c.   *Native language-speakers.* Language, and with it indigeneity, matters a lot. Even when we control for other variables that are correlated with language such as geographic location, native language-speaking households still fell behind Spanish-speaking households (-0.10 percent in the full sample).

d.   *Basic infrastructure.* We find evidence of increasing returns to the number of services households command. This results stands in all three iterations of the regression. In the full sample, holding all other influences constant, if a household had access to one of four services (telephone, electricity, water, sanitation) in 1994, this increased the per capita growth rate by 0.04 percent (insignificant). If the household had access to two services, per capita growth was, on average, 0.05 percent higher (the marginal return on the second service is 0.01 percent). However, marginal returns increase: the third service has a marginal return of 0.11 percent and the fourth service of 0.12 percent. Electricity is the most important service linked to household welfare improvements in rural areas and a telephone in urban areas.

e.   *Household size.* Household size influences welfare developments. Results from regressions of the *full sample* as well as the restricted samples suggest that (i) larger households fare worse than smaller ones; and (ii) this relationship is not linear; the larger the household, the lower the additional reduction in welfare. Additionally, we find that the dependency ratio (number non-income earners to income earners) has a marginally significant independent negative influence on household per capita consumption growth (in most restricted sample only). The relationship between household size and welfare developments requires further study since it is not apparent why larger households (independent from the dependency ratio) should have lower welfare increases than smaller households.

f.   *Education and experience.* The higher the education (and the more work experience) of the household head in 1994, the larger the growth in per capita expenditures. This mirrors the common observation in Peru that the better educated and more experienced have progressed relatively more than the less educated in recent years. One more year of education increased the household per capita consumption growth rate by 0.03 percent.

g.   *Financial savings.* Households that commanded financial savings in both 1994 and 1997 achieved higher welfare growth rates (0.20 percent).

h.   *Households with home-based businesses.* Both urban and rural households that stated that they used at least one room in their house for business purposes were better off than households that did not have this possibility. These households often had informal earning possibilities. This result holds when controlling for all other factors that influence consumption growth.

Table A1.1: Panel Growth Regression

Source	SS	df	MS			
Model	109.423594	15	7.29490627			
Residual	187.377249	875	.214145428			
Total	296.800843	890	.333484094			

Number of obs = 891
F(15, 875) = 34.07
Prob > F = 0.0000
R-squared = 0.3687
Adj R-squared = 0.3579
Root MSE = .46276

19794c	Coef.	Std. Err.	t	P>|t|	[95% Conf. Interval]	
lgpcr94b	-.6895338	.031891	-21.622	0.000	-.7521257	-.626942
yrsh	.0311574	.0043992	7.083	0.000	.0225232	.0397915
quechua	-.0951024	.0402248	-2.364	0.018	-.1740507	-.0161541
edadh	.0058017	.0012675	4.577	0.000	.003314	.0082893
female	.108005	.0449603	2.402	0.017	.0197625	.1962475
famtam	-.1021141	.027817	-3.671	0.000	-.1567099	-.0475183
famtam2	.0048443	.0020883	2.320	0.021	.0007457	.008943
econroom	.1494465	.0403158	3.707	0.000	.0703196	.2285734
ahfin4y7	.2040275	.090935	2.244	0.025	.0255512	.3825037
migroh	.0457797	.0321832	1.422	0.155	-.0173855	.108945
drt94	-.0091593	.009849	-0.930	0.353	-.0284898	.0101712
s1	.0417148	.0527044	0.791	0.429	-.061727	.1451566
s2	.0541988	.0558559	0.970	0.332	-.0554285	.163826
s3	.163079	.0498228	3.273	0.001	.0652929	.2608651
s4	.2769414	.0695599	3.981	0.000	.1404177	.4134651
_cons	5.117684	.2790731	18.338	0.000	4.569953	5.665414

<u>Variable Names</u>: 'lgpcr94b' log of consumption per capita in 1994; 'yrsh': years of education of the household head in 1994; 'quechua': household head reports quechua as mother tongue in 1994; 'edadh': age of the household head 1994; 'female': dummy variable for headship of household being 1 if female household head in 1994; famtam: household size 1994; famtam2: household size squared 1994; 'econroom': dummy variable being 1 for households that used at least one room in their house for business purposes in 1994; 'ahfin4y7' dummy variable being 1 for households that had financial savings in both 1994 and 1997; 'migroh': dummy variable for migrants being 1 if the household head was not born in the same location than he/she lived in 1994; 'drt94': dependency ratio in 1994 defined as ratio of income earners to non-income earners; 's1' : dummy variable for households that had one service (water, electricity, sanitation, telephone) in 1994; 's2': dummy variable for households that had two services in 1994; 's3': dummy variable for households that had three services in 1994; 's4': dummy variable for households that had four services in 1994; _cons: constant term.

ANNEX II: METHODOLOGY

Introduction

Peru is one of the countries that pioneered comprehensive household surveys aimed at measuring poverty and well-being. The first Living Standard Measurement Survey (LSMS) in Peru was conducted in 1985 by the National Statistical Institute (INEI) and since then the Instituto Cuánto has conducted a host of other surveys. While each survey added or modified several questions, partly because of the specific interest of funding organizations, the core of the surveys, with their focus on housing conditions, education, health, migration, the labor market, and agricultural activity, has stayed remarkably constant. The two most recent and largest Cuánto surveys are those used in this study: the 1994 and 1997 *Encuestas de Niveles de Vida* (ENNIV). They employed a sample frame to achieve representability in the urban and rural areas of the three agro-climatic zones in the country (Coast, Sierra, Selva) plus Lima.

Working with household survey data requires many - often cumbersome - steps of data cleaning and consistency checks before the actual empirical investigations can begin. Especially when comparing different variables over time, one of our primary aims, caution is necessary. And this statement holds even more when the aim is to compare an artificially created variable between surveys. For poverty analysis this variable is central as we first have to derive a monetary welfare measure (consumption or income). Further, the monetary aggregate need to be deflated over both time and space. And then the (in)famous poverty lines need to be derived before the simplest of all comparisons - calculating headcount rates - can take place. Along the way, many assumptions have to be made.

This annex contains a description of how we used the two LSMS surveys from the Instituto Cuánto. We start with a short background section on poverty comparisons in general, which stresses the importance of defining welfare in a consistent manner when conducting comparisons over time. We then describe how we aggregated consumption expenditures, paying particular attention to their comparability between the two survey years. Income definitions are also included. We next explain how we derived poverty lines for 1994 and 1997 and the necessary price adjustments. Finally, we report the results of several sensitivity analyses with respect to adult equivalence and economies of scale.

Background: Poverty Comparisons in Time

One of our aims when analyzing the 1994 and 1997 Living Standard Measurement Surveys was to compare poverty and welfare changes of the Peruvian population over time. At face value this does not seem to be very difficult. Both surveys include household income and consumption that can be converted into per capita terms and then compared to certain absolute standards, the poverty lines. Headcount rates, poverty gaps, and poverty severity can be calculated and compared in reference to these poverty lines over time.

But for a number of reasons, poverty comparisons using consecutive surveys are generally quite cumbersome and difficult. First of all, it has to be ensured that the sampling frame (from which factor expansions are computed) is the same for the two years and that the definitions which determine the sampling process are identical. For example, if stratification of the sample is conducted with respect to urban and rural areas, the latter needs to be defined in the same way in consecutive years. The same holds for other stratified variables, be they of a political or socio-economic nature. For example, in addition to the nationally representative household surveys mentioned above, Cuánto also fielded one relatively small survey in 1996. This was a pure panel survey, as all 1,491 households interviewed were also part of the larger 1994 survey. While statements can be made about the comparison of poverty between 1994 and 1996 for *the panel households*,[50] generalizations for the whole country cannot be made. Even if the selection of the panel had been completely random (i.e., all households forming part of the 1994 survey had the same chance of being selected for the panel), the 1996 survey would not have been nationally representative. Newly formed households after 1994 had a zero probability of being selected in the 1996 survey. Although the bias between two years might be small, its effect cannot be quantified.

Second, poverty comparisons are based on a number of very stringent assumptions. The most common method of conducting poverty comparisons is to base all nominal income and consumption data from different surveys on one time period and one region; i.e., to deflate nominal variables in space and time and hence convert them into real values.[51] These real values are then compared to a constant poverty line representing a minimum consumption basket. Generally, the basket itself (at least the food basket) is derived from actual consumption patterns of the poor so that it is appropriate for the type of analysis being carried out. This basket of goods is supposed to present a certain welfare level that can be compared across households. One of the important assumptions underlying such welfare comparisons is that households have the same tastes; i.e., that the welfare households derive from consuming the basic bundle of commodities is identical. Although this is an idealization, we can nevertheless think of the basic bundle of goods as a yardstick against which we measure people's (relative) welfare - we express the (relative) welfare of households as how many times can they consume a given bundle of goods.

Welfare comparisons over time leave, if at all possible, this yardstick (or basic basket of goods) constant. Hence, the composition of the food basket with all its components of fruits, vegetables, meats, etc., is kept constant, as is the non-food components such as housing, clothing, services, the use of durable items, and the like. However, as the assumption of identical tastes was a shortcut, so is this. Over time, relative prices among goods change. Households adjust to these relative price changes by choosing a different mix of commodities, generally increasing the consumption of relatively cheaper products and reducing intake of relatively more expensive ones. A basket of goods that was representative of the poor's consumption pattern in a base period hence is not necessarily representative of the consumption pattern in a different time period. Both relative price changes and modifications in preferences can account for such shifting consumption patterns. Welfare comparisons using a fixed basket in time hence are - again - only approximations.[52]

---

[50] Instituto Cuánto (1997) produced a study comparing poverty in the 1994-1996 panel and was careful not to generalize results to the whole of Peru.

[51] See, for example, Ferreira and Litchfield (1998)

[52] This study uses a fixed basket of total goods (food and non-food goods alike) to derive poverty lines and conduct poverty comparisons. This differs markedly from the traditional poverty analysis in Peru, which keeps only the food basket constant over time and derived the non-food component endogenously.

Third, as mentioned above, careful price deflation is crucial. A number of different methods have been used in past studies to derive spatial and time indices in order to make consumption expenditures comparable among households in different locations and of different survey years. But all of them require the availability of regionally distinct price indices for broad product groups. In many countries such information does not exist. In Peru, however, detailed price information exists for food products in all regions and for non-food categories in 25 urban centers. As will be shown, we can use this information to adjust nominal consumption in all survey years.

Fourth, if the basket of goods is kept constant over time, the definition of consumption needs to be the same as well. Poverty measurement can be seriously distorted if the definition of consumption changes over time. For example, consecutive surveys might add a question on expenditures and auto-consumption of a very specific food item that was not asked for before. Obviously, even if the true food consumption of households is completely identical in the two survey years, it would appear on paper to be higher in the year in which the additional question was asked. If the basket of goods against which we compare consumption expenditures of households is fixed, however, adding further consumption items will lead to an unequivocal reduction in poverty.[53]

Caution also needs to be taken if the meaning or phrasing of questions in the consumption module changes over time. Even if items for which households are asked to report expenditures or auto-consumption are identical, the phrasing of questions can have a profound impact on the level and structure of responses. An example from the Cuánto surveys 1994 and 1997 is used below to illustrate this point.

Finally, poverty comparisons should ideally establish whether or not observed trends in statistics are robust. This would imply varying some of the underlying procedures for consumption aggregation, such as imputation procedures or testing the effect of implicit assumptions about economies of scale or adult equivalence scales. Further, the poverty line can also be varied over a wide range of different values to test whether the choice of poverty line matters for the direction of welfare changes.

---

53 Lanjouw and Lanjouw (1997) show that if consumption questions change over time so that the definition simply cannot be held constant, a second possibility is to keep only the food basket constant and derive the non-food basket implicitly by calculating the Engel coefficient. They show that this will give consistent estimates of poverty under a number of assumptions, including a homogenous relationship between food expenditures and total expenditures. Further, between the survey years little or no relative price changes between food and non-food goods should occur.

Defining Welfare

Consumption

The consumption aggregate we are using is designed to be comparable for the 1994 and 1997 survey years. Although the surveys show a very high degree of homogeneity, the questionnaire did change in several ways: new products were added, product groups were changed, separate products in one year were summed up in the next year, and questions were reformulated which gave them a different meaning.

We also made many small adjustments in almost all components of the consumption aggregate. Table 1 contains the description for different product categories and the consumption definition we used (computer programs are available on request).[54] As can be seen, certain exclusions and inclusions of sub-components were made in the education, health, semi-durable, transfer and auto-consumption sections (from own business). We could not include the depreciation stream from durable consumer goods because the 1994 survey did not include the age structure of the household durable consumer goods, which meant that depreciation rates could not be calculated.[55] Similarly, furniture purchases were not included. The food, rent and social program modules require more elaborate explanation.

Food Module. While the food module of the questionnaire appears to be almost completely identical in 1994 and 1997, Cuánto introduced one considerable modification. Specifically, Cuánto added one supplementary question to the food module in 1997 which reads *total autoconsumo y autosuministro*. The consequence of including this well-intentioned question was that more than one third of all sample households and their interviewers (close to 1,300) chose to respond *only* to the aggregate question - thereby avoiding detailed answers. Generally, it has been shown that detailed consumption questions have a clear advantage over aggregate questions as they help respondents to recollect quantities and expenditures better. Lanjouw (1997) reports that under-declaration can be significant in shorter questionnaires, especially for lower-income groups.

---

[54] Send email to Jhentschel@worldbank.org.

[55] The 1997 survey includes this age structure. Current consumption from the stock of durable goods can then be estimated (the median age can be calculated for each type of good assuming that the depreciation rate is half the life duration of the products). Given the age of individual products per household, one could individually compute the expected remaining life of each product.

Table A2.1.: Definition of the Consumption Aggregate, 1994 and 1997

Item	1997	1994
Consumer durables	Excluded	excluded
Daily non-food, Other	all purchase and auto-consumption included (Z3A, Z3B) except for expenditures on public telephones, as not in 1994 (z2=109)	all purchases and auto-consumption
In-kind consumption from firm/business	Includes auto-consumption from firms (W19)	Included
In-kind consumption from work	Primary and secondary work over last 7 days, primary and secondary work over last 12 months (adjusted for time period worked) (M11B, M12B, O11B, O12B, R12B, R13B, T12B, T13B)	included as in 1997 (identical questions)
Education	direct expenditures in education section included (F10A, F10B, F10C, F10D, F10E)	school uniforms excluded (as included in the services sections). Also, 1997 questionnaire asked for frequencies but 1994 survey did not. Hence, we used median frequencies from the 1997 survey for evaluating payment of matriculation, books, transport in 1994. Also, a separate questions on expenditure for children under age 6 in 1994 surveys excluded because not in 1997 survey.
Furniture	Excluded (and depreciation rate cannot be calculated)	Excluded
Food module	Purchases and valued autoconsumption (AE4, AE5, AE6 and AE7) included	purchases and valued auto-consumption (identical apart from minor and negligible different grouping); however, an additional question which allowed households to only give one aggregate figure for total food purchases did cause comparability problems (see text).
Health expenditures	direct health expenditure in health section included (H11A, H11B, H15, H19); but excluded in services section (AA1=125,126,127) as recall period different and not clear if these are additional or the same products mentioned in the health section	same as 1997: expenditures in health section included, in service section excluded. However, examining the share of health expenditure in total expenditure, we found a number (61)of outlier households which stated that they spent more of 50 percent of their total expenditure on health. This did not happen in 1997. Hence, we excluded these outliers.
House expenditures	water (D9A), light (D12A), heating and cooking fuel (D14A), telephone (D18B and D20A), municipal fees (D22A) [note: municipal arbitration excluded]	all included
Payments for house (repayment of credit)	Excluded	Excluded
Rent	Excluded (questions different). See explanation in text.	excluded (questions different). See explanation in text.
Semi-durables and services	only purchase included as the 1994 questionnaire did not include auto-consumption	only purchase included;
Social programs	only food aid included as 1994 survey did not ask for other social program transfers; excludes 'alimento por trabajo' ah1=506 as not in 1994 survey	food aid included (as captured in the food section under aj02=327 and ak02=327); excludes al01=09 as Cuánto maintains that question al01=09 was imputed into aj03=327
Transfer expenditures	Ceremonies (AD1=02), direct taxes (AD1=03), social security (AD1=04), membership fees (AD1=07), donations (AD1=09). Insurance questions excluded as not in 1994 survey (AD1=06).	ceremonies (in 1994 in services module), social security, membership fees, donations, direct taxes

While we do find a pattern in responses when comparing the food share of households answering the detailed questionnaire with the food share of households that only give one aggregate food expenditure value, we have opted not to adjust this variable. Table A2.2 shows that the foodshare of households answering the detailed questions tends to be significantly higher than the foodshare of households giving only one, aggregate estimate for the richest three quintiles. We opted, however, not to make adjustments for two reasons: (a) in the lowest two quintiles (which are our

Table A2.2: Detailed and Aggregate Food Module Responses		
quintile	foodshare of households answering detailed questions	foodshare of households answering aggregate question
1	67.9	68.1
2	60.3	60.2
3	56.2	53.4
4	49.7	47.9
5	43.9	39.2

Source: ENNIV (1997), own calculations. Population quintiles defined by total real expenditures.

primary concern in a poverty study), the mean difference is not very large; and (b) it is extremely difficult to make an adjustment as the percentage of total expenditure spent on food shows enormous fluctuations across households in one quintile (this is generally observed in household surveys, see Lanjouw and Lanjouw 1997). It is therefore questionable to fix the foodshare, which accounts for the bulk of expenditures, to an average number across households.

Rent. Next to food, the actual (or imputed) rental value of the house tends to be the most important budget item for the poor and non-poor alike. We therefore were very eager to include this variable in our consumption aggregate, as it adds an important welfare component of families: how much space households have, whether the house is made of weather-resistant material, how close the shelter is from the nearest market, what transportation possibilities exist. All such factors enter into the determinants of the housing value, which we were eager to incorporate, albeit ensuring that we have consistency over the years.

Both the 1994 and 1997 surveys collected information on (a) actual rent paid; and (b) self-estimated imputed rent from the households that were owner-occupiers. Two problems arose here. First, we had to undertake some simple imputations of the value of housing. These had to be carried out for those households that provided neither actual nor estimated rental value of their housing. For this purpose, we used simple hedonic regressions in which we postulated the value of housing to be a function of the stock of assets of the household, regional dummies (capturing price variations), and both housing (material, size) and household (size) characteristics. Based on their housing, household, and asset characteristics, we predicted housing expenditures for those households that did not report a value for the actual or estimated rental value of their house - 238 households in 1994 and 13 in 1997.

The second problem that arose was much more severe. The questionnaire had changed between the two survey years so we needed to test whether we could indeed include rental values of the house without compromising the comparability between the surveys. While both surveys had a question recording the *actual* rent paid by households, the 1994 survey had a follow-up question for owner-occupiers in which households were asked how much they would *charge* if they were to rent their house. In contrast, the 1997 questionnaire queried owner-occupiers how much they would be willing to *pay* had they to rent their own house. Our initial hypothesis was that the change in the question would have only a marginal impact on the structure and level of this variable.

We conducted several tests to explore whether the rent sections were comparable. The first one involved the imputation regressions reported above. As Lanjouw et al (1996) have shown, such imputation regressions can be used to predict housing prices in different regions of the country while controlling for the quality and characteristics of housing. The idea is simple: using the median values for all exogenous variables (asset variables, housing and household characteristics, geographic dummy variables) and the estimated parameter values, we derived the expected price of a standard house in all regions for 1994. Using the *same* median values of the exogenous variables (as we want to control for quality over time) but now employing parameter estimates for 1997, we could calculate rental values for 1997 as well (as this is when the change in the questionnaire took place). While the change in the housing price itself is interesting, we can now also add one more control variable, as INEI, the Peruvian Statistical Institute, compiles a value for housing (*alquiler*) for 25 cities in the country. Table A2.3 shows the results for the change between June 1994 and October 1997 (the months of the surveys). According to the regional INEI price data, all urban regions experienced considerably slower rent inflation than (implicitly) recorded in the surveys.

Table A2.3: Rental Values in 1994 and 1997				
Area	Predicted Rental Value, 1994 (soles per year)	Predicted Rental Value, 1997 (soles per year)	Change in Predicted Value, 1994/97 (%)	Change in Rental Index, INEI (%)
Lima	1701	2593	52.4	34.2
Coast Urban	1184	1822	53.9	35.5
Coast Rural	221	445	101.4	-
Sierra Urban	731	1452	98.6	35.9
Sierra Rural	144	537	272.9	-
Selva Urban	764	1371	79.5	26.7
Selva Rural	200	372	86.0	-

Source: Staff estimates based on ENNIV 1994 and 1997; INEI Regional Offices.

The second possibility to test the change in the rental variable over time was to look at how the *same* households evaluated their rental value in 1994 and 1997. In line with its tradition, Cuánto included in its 1997 sample about 900 households that had already been interviewed in 1994. We divided this panel dataset into 10 rent deciles; i.e., the households reporting the lowest rental values were grouped in decile 1, the households with the highest in decile 10. Using a transition matrix, we could then see how this ranking of households with respect to the rent variable changes. Since the households live in the same dwelling for both survey years, we would assume that the ranking of households stays very stable if the different question does not have an impact on their reporting patterns. However, we find that rankings changed considerably: only about 25 percent of the panel sample were located on the diagonal in the transition matrix, which implies that they did not change their decile ranking between 1994 and 1997. An additional 25 percent were off by one decile but roughly half of the total sample showed changes of at least two decile rankings, which implies significant ranking changes - although these are identical households living in the same dwellings in 1994 and 1997.

Finally, we looked at the overall expenditure composition. Our hypothesis was that the change in the questionnaire would likely lead to a lower share in households' subjective evaluation of their rental value in 1997 compared to 1994 (since in 1997 households were asked what they would pay for their own house in rent). But this did not prove to be the case - actually, the share of total expenditure on (actual and self-declared) rent increased marginally over the 1994-1997 period (from 14 to 16 percent). However, this average does mark quite large variations in rental value between the years: actual and imputed rent was a variable with a very high fluctuation as a share of total expenditures - rent patterns almost reversed in certain regions. Table A2.4 tabulates the changing food- and rentshare of total expenditures between 1994 and 1997. Table A2.4 also shows that the variation in the foodshare between 1994 and 1997 is significantly reduced if rent is excluded as a component of total consumption.

Given these findings, we concluded that changing the question regarding the rent variable had a significant impact on responses and, especially, their structure in different expenditure groups. Since one of our main aims was welfare comparison, we therefore chose to exclude the rental value from the consumption aggregation. The income definition also did not include the rental value.

Food Donations. The questionnaire also changed considerably between 1994 and 1997 with respect to how food donations are treated. In 1994, these were not explicitly asked for but incorporated into two different questions. First, in the section on food consumption, households entered the value of prepared food products.[56] Second, households were asked how much income or value in products they received from non-profit organizations (examples given in the questionnaire were *Vaso de Leche*, *Club de Madre* and CARITAS).[57] Cuánto holds that the value of food donations was actually *included* in the prepared food question in the food module when the original data were processed. The questionnaire was considerably different in 1997. Cuánto added an entire section on access to social services in which households reported the value of food received by program and funding source. In addition, the food module continued to include the same question that had been asked in 1994; i.e., the value of prepared food products consumed by the household.

---

[56]   This is in the food module section in 1994, variables aj02 and ak02 (rubrique 327).

[57]   This refers to code al01=09 in the 1994 questionnaire.

Table A2.4: Expenditure Patterns and Consumption Definition

Area	Quintile	Including Imputed Rent				Excluding Imputed Rent		
		Foodshare 1994	Foodshare 1997	d(Foodshare) 1994/1997	d(Rentshare) 1994/97	Foodshare 1994	Foodshare 1997	d(Foodshare) 1994-1997
Lima	1	56.84	50.13	-6.71	1.64	66.6	59.95	-6.65
	2	52.75	48.29	-4.46	-0.30	63.36	57.8	-5.56
	3	50.27	47.2	-3.07	-0.77	61.68	57.38	-4.30
	4	45.99	41.08	-4.91	-0.44	58.31	51.44	-6.87
	5	34.21	33.18	-1.03	-5.91	49.2	43.81	-5.39
Coast	1	56.95	49.45	-7.50	8.09	64.98	62.78	-2.20
Urban	2	52.86	47.93	-4.93	4.13	61.89	59.09	-2.80
	3	50.55	48.7	-1.85	1.51	60.75	59.37	-1.38
	4	47.82	44.9	-2.92	0.85	57.87	54.89	-2.98
	5	39.22	42.11	2.89	-2.03	49.77	52.39	2.62
Coast	1	71.88	69.2	-2.68	-0.02	78.66	75.78	-2.88
Rural	2	68.52	68.39	-0.13	-0.87	74.39	73.51	-0.88
	3	68.24	67.28	-0.96	0.58	73.46	72.72	-0.74
	4	59.76	63.98	4.22	-0.47	64.85	69.05	4.20
	5	57.42	58.82	1.40	-1.30	63.49	63.98	0.49
Sierra	1	58.91	48.9	-10.01	4.84	66.93	59	-7.93
Urban	2	56.64	47.13	-9.51	4.23	63.82	56.04	-7.78
	3	48.3	46.49	-1.81	1.39	56.68	55.81	-0.87
	4	48	42.92	-5.08	2.28	57.52	52.79	-4.73
	5	41.89	40.76	-1.13	-1.15	52.65	50.65	-2.00
Sierra	1	72	69.28	-2.72	2.45	78.69	78.17	-0.52
Rural	2	71.43	64.93	-6.50	6.40	76.45	74.64	-1.81
	3	69.43	64.93	-4.50	3.90	75.12	73.33	-1.79
	4	69.87	63.95	-5.92	3.85	74.3	70.9	-3.40
	5	62.98	63.4	0.42	0.13	69.44	69.73	0.29
Selva	1	63.02	52.59	-10.43	11.27	70.06	66.74	-3.32
Urban	2	61.65	55.57	-6.08	6.71	69.6	68.02	-1.58
	3	56.39	52.68	-3.71	4.11	63.59	62.59	-1.00
	4	53.08	50.46	-2.62	0.70	62.56	60.23	-2.33
	5	46.48	47.33	0.85	-1.43	56.07	56.35	0.28
Selva	1	72.76	68.66	-4.10	0.32	81.08	76.74	-4.34
Rural	2	73.56	68.24	-5.32	1.50	78.98	74.56	-4.42
	3	67.36	65.16	-2.20	0.28	72.69	70.6	-2.09
	4	67.88	67.49	-0.39	-0.50	73.22	72.33	-0.89
	5	68.89	64.5	-4.39	-0.13	74.17	69.28	-4.89

Source: Staff estimates based on ENNIV (1994, 1997).

Comparing the 1994 and 1997 surveys shows considerable changes in the value of food donations recorded by the household survey. In 1997 prices, total estimated food donations in 1994 were 180 million soles,[58] while the total estimated benefits of food programs was 1.3 billion soles in 1997.[59] These are low estimates for 1994 but very high estimates for 1997.

We included food donations in a different form than Cuánto for 1997. First and most important, Cuánto multiplied daily food donation receipts by 365 to obtain annual values. However, several of the donation programs do not work every day per week and certainly not all weeks per year. The most important one is the school breakfast program which operates from Monday to Friday and about 2/3 of the whole year. Also, *comedores populares* and *Club de Madre* food distribution points are generally operated from Monday to Friday, and sometimes also on Saturday. Second, it becomes clear studying the data that many responding households were confused as to whether they were supposed to give the (a) daily value of donations received; or (b) the value for the entire recall period. For example, many households responded that they obtained five times a Glass of Milk for two children in a recall period of a week and they listed 10 soles as the value they received. Obviously, the value must refer to the *total* of the five times two milk rations received rather than to a single glass (10 soles was about 4 dollars at the time of the survey). In its estimates, Cuánto interpreted these 10 soles as the *daily* value of one glass of milk, which was received 365 times a year - hence adding about US$1,600 to the expenditure of the particular households. In our approach, we calculated the median value of one glass of milk or school lunch per region and used this value to estimate the value of these items for the households. We assumed that schools operate five times a week and 8 months a year. The Glass of Milk program was assumed to work 5 times a week during the whole year. Making these adjustments, our estimate of total food aid in 1997 dropped from 1.3 billion soles (Cuánto) to 800 billion soles – a figure much more in line with expenditure reports of the large nutrition programs.[60]

As shown in the main body of this study when discussing social expenditures, the inclusion or exclusion of food aid has a marked impact on calculated poverty rates, especially in the rural highlands. The severe poverty rate would have been three percent higher had we excluded the donations. Poverty calculations are quite sensitive to changes in definitions here, and further in-depth analyses from other researchers would be welcome.

---

[58] The survey code in 1994 is al02=09.

[59] The survey codes in 1997 are ah1=501-505, 507-508.

[60] For the measurement of welfare and poverty, a problem nevertheless remains since there seems to have been an underestimation of food donations in 1994. Hence, we are overestimating welfare improvements by including food aid. On the other hand, had we left food donations aside while in reality they had increased, we would have underestimated welfare increases.

Income

For the inequality comparisons, we use a definition of income similar to that of Cuánto except in one important aspect: To maintain comparability in income definitions between 1994 and 1997, we prefer to use monetary income. Monetary income includes four clearly defined income categories (self-employed income, wages, transfers and property income). Monetary income excludes self-consumption, imputed rent, and some miscellaneous income categories as defined by Cuánto. The latter three categories appear to be less comparable between 1994 and 1997 for two reasons. First, there are differences in the questions asked, and they are important in calculating self-consumption and imputed rent. Second, Cuánto has different definitions of total income for each year. For example, payments to social security on behalf of the employee do not appear in both years. In terms of income levels, the exclusion of imputed rent makes the biggest difference in estimating new income levels because imputed rent is such a large component of Cuánto income definitions.[61] Imputed rent represented around 12 to 15 percent of family income (in nominal soles, imputed rent corresponded to $1,674 out of a weighted average income of $11,071 in 1994; and, $2,065 out of an weighted average income of $17,924 in 1997).

Poverty Lines & Price Deflation

Food Basket and Value in 1994. The Cuánto surveys did not collect quantity or price information in the consumption module. This has important implications for the derivation of poverty lines: it implies that the composition of the basic food basket cannot be derived from the survey itself and has to be obtained from an external source. We use the basic food basket from Cuánto (see Moncada and Webb 1996) as the starting point of our analysis. It is priced in 1994 and 1997 using detailed regional price indices supplied by the Statistical Institute, INEI.

Non-Food Basket and Value in 1994, Poverty Line in 1994. Different from common practice in Peru, we keep the basket of non-food goods constant over time. This approach has been suggested several times by Francke (1997) and goes back to the argument made earlier that ideally we want to fix a certain welfare level (associated with a fixed bundle of goods) over time. In international practice, this seems to be the preferred way of performing welfare comparisons in time (Ferreira and Litchfield 1998, MacIsaac and Hentschel 1996, Ravallion 1994). We use 1994 as the reference year to derive the basic consumption bundle. We employ the values of three normative food baskets used in Peru and their value and then derive the upper bound poverty lines. For this we use as a reference group the population that spends on food exactly at the value of the food poverty line. The *total* expenditure of this group then becomes the upper bound poverty line. Weights for the non-food basket can be consequently derived (Table A2.5).

Poverty Lines in 1997. The food and non-food baskets from 1994 were then priced in 1997 using data from INEI regional offices. We computed price indices for non-food categories from price information provided by INEI for 26 cities in the Sierra, Coast, Selva

---

[61] The figures on inequality presented in the main body of this study also do not take into account other non-cash income.

and Lima. For each region, we calculated the average price index and used it to value the 1994 basket in 1997. Since INEI reports only urban prices, we assumed that the relative price rise (not its absolute level) between rural and urban areas in all regions is the same between the survey years.

Category	Weights 1994	Annual Value, 1994 (June 1994 prices)	Inflation Oct. 97/June 94	Annual Value, 1997 (Oct. 1997 prices)
Lima				
food	0.630	911.04	1.30[2]	1182.38
clothing	0.049	70.67	1.37	96.60
water, electricity	0.086	125.05	1.44	179.58
cleaning	0.027	39.12	1.38	53.78
health	0.075	108.33	1.56	169.43
transport	0.075	108.33	1.37	148.20
education	0.055	80.12	1.54	123.39
other	0.004	11.44	1.31	14.99
[poverty line]		1,454.10		1968.34
Urban Coast				
food	0.610	789.13	1.31[2]	1032.75
clothing	0.028	35.95	1.28	45.83
water, electricity	0.111	143.91	1.36	195.00
cleaning	0.031	39.97	1.23	49.28
health	0.052	66.96	1.42	94.75
transport	0.065	83.83	1.23	102.78
education	0.061	79.55	1.45	115.66
other	0.043	58.40	1.29	75.16
[poverty line]		1,297.70		1,711.22
Rural Coast				
food	0.660	700.07	1.31[2]	917.47
clothing	0.068	72.67	1.28	92.66
water, electricity	0.041	44.03	1.36	59.66
cleaning	0.027	29.18	1.23	35.97
health	0.066	70.32	1.42	99.50
transport	0.064	67.86	1.23	83.20
education	0.032	33.88	1.45	49.26
other	0.043	50.69	1.29	65.24
[poverty line]		1,068.70		1,402.96
Urban Sierra				
food	0.610	668.68	1.30[2]	866.45
clothing	0.049	53.58	1.29	69.32
water, electricity	0.105	116.00	1.36	157.60
cleaning	0.029	31.82	1.23	39.24
health	0.046	50.60	1.42	71.96
transport	0.054	59.44	1.29	76.59
education	0.079	86.73	1.47	127.42
other	0.030	37.95	1.31	49.76
[poverty line]		1,104.80		1,458.34
Rural Sierra				
food	0.760	583.23	1.36[2]	791.48
clothing	0.063	48.03	1.29	62.14
water, electricity	0.029	22.56	1.36	30.65
cleaning	0.034	26.17	1.23	32.26
health	0.037	28.24	1.42	40.16
transport	0.026	19.80	1.29	25.51
education	0.025	19.49	1.47	28.63
other	0.026	19.79	1.31	25.95
[poverty line]		767.30		1,036.78

Table A2.5. Derivation of Poverty Lines[1], 1994, 1997

Category	Weights 1994	Value 1994	Inflation Oct-97/June-94	Value 1997
Urban Selva				
food	0.650	702.99	1.31[2]	922.57
clothing	0.049	53.18	1.20	63.71
water, electricity	0.097	104.10	1.27	131.79
cleaning	0.032	33.91	1.20	40.76
health	0.051	54.79	1.42	77.80
transport	0.043	55.33	1.26	69.83
education	0.043	45.75	1.34	61.22
other	0.028	26.45	1.20	31.60
[poverty line]		**1,076.50**		**1,399.27**
Rural Selva				
food	0.730	647.51	1.36[2]	880.23
clothing	0.064	57.37	1.20	68.73
water, electricity	0.018	15.61	1.27	19.77
cleaning	0.047	42.02	1.20	50.51
health	0.049	44.07	1.42	62.58
transport	0.050	44.16	1.26	55.73
education	0.018	15.61	1.34	20.89
other	0.025	25.83	1.20	30.87
[poverty line]		**892.20**		**1,189.31**

1   Poverty lines in all years are derived using the poverty basket of the year 1994. Consumption is defined as outlined in the previous section (e.g., total consumption excludes rental value of the home); product group definitions follow the Instituto Cuánto. The food share in 1994 (by region) is determined by the decile of the population that spends on food products the value of the exogenously determined food basket (Moncada 1996). Expenditure shares in 1994 refer to this population group. We calculated price changes for non-food categories between two survey years using INEI city price indices by broad product group for 26 cities, calculating average indices by region. Since INEI reports only urban prices, we assume that the price rises (not their absolute level) in rural areas are the same as in their urban counterparts.

2   Price index of the exogenously given food basket derived from dividing the nominal value of the basket in different years. The value of the food basket in all regions in 1994 and 1997 was calculated by the Instituto Cuánto.

Price Deflation. Two price deflations were applied. First, we deflated prices over time, to adjust all nominal expenditure values in the 1994 survey to the month of June and all nominal expenditures in the 1997 survey to the month of October. Such adjustment for inflation was carried out by Cuánto and is included in the basic database. Second, rather than working with seven different poverty lines, we adjusted all household consumption (and income) values to the price of Lima. For this exercise we used the computed poverty lines and price deflators, defining Lima as "1" and using the ratio between the Lima poverty line and each individual regional poverty line as a deflator for regional monetary values. This allowed us to compare welfare levels among households directly.

Definition of Severe Poverty Line. The lower or severe poverty line used in the report is not strictly comparable to the extreme poverty line used in most other poverty studies. This is for a simple reason. As outlined at length above, we had to exclude several important consumption components from our aggregate in order to achieve comparability between the 1994 and 1997 surveys. Most important of these exclusions was the rent value. The definition of the extreme poverty line is generally the value of the food basket alone. Extreme poverty rates would then be the percentage of the population whose total expenditures is not enough to purchase such a basic food basket. However, if we were to apply this definition here, extreme poverty rates would be severely inflated since our total consumption aggregate is lower due to the exclusion of the rent. Therefore, we opted to apply an arbitrary severe poverty line that nevertheless has the property of being perfectly comparable across time. We chose two-thirds of the upper poverty line (at Lima prices) as this rate.

Regional Poverty Estimates and Standard Errors

As pointed out at the beginning of this study, poverty estimates derived from household surveys are not 'exact' but carry a certain degree of insecurity as they are derived for a fraction of the total population of the country. Tables A2.6 and A2.7 record the standard and severe poverty statistics (headcount rate, poverty gap and poverty severity) by geographical region for 1994 and 1997, including the estimated standard errors that take into account stratification and clustering of sample design.

| Area | Headcount Rate | | Poverty Gap | | Poverty Severity | |
	1994	1997	1994	1997	1994	1997
PERU	53.5	49.0	18.9	15.9	9.1	6.9
	(1.3)	(1.2)	(0.7)	(0.6)	(0.4)	(0.3)
Lima	42.2	34.1	11.5	8.5	4.6	3.1
	(2.4)	(2.1)	(0.9)	(0.8)	(0.4)	(0.4)
Coast Urban	51.9	52.8	17.7	16.8	8.2	7.1
	(3.8)	(3.5)	(1.8)	(1.5)	(1.0)	(0.8)
Coast Rural	64.4	62.1	25.7	22.5	12.9	10.6
	(4.9)	(4.9)	(3.1)	(2.4)	(2.1)	(1.4)
Sierra Urban	48.1	36.2	16.6	11.6	8.0	5.1
	(3.9)	(3.6)	(1.9)	(1.6)	(1.1)	(0.8)
Sierra Rural	65.9	64.6	26.6	23.5	16.9	10.9
	(2.8)	(2.8)	(1.5)	(1.6)	(1.1)	(0.9)
Selva Urban	43.0	42.9	13.6	12.9	5.8	5.3
	(3.9)	(3.7)	(1.8)	(1.2)	(0.9)	(0.6)
Selva Rural	72.1	66.9	29.7	24.3	15.3	11.5
	(3.0)	(3.3)	(2.3)	(2.2)	(1.6)	(1.4)

Table A2.6: *Poverty: Statistics and Standard Errors, by Region, 1994 and 1997*

<u>Source</u>: Staff estimates based on ENNIV (1994, 1997).

Table A2.7: Severe Poverty: Statistics and Standard Errors, by Region, 1994 and 1997

Area	Headcount Rate		Poverty Gap		Poverty Severity	
	1994	1997	1994	1997	1994	1997
PERU	18.8	14.8	5.0	3.2	2.0	1.0
	(1.0	(0.9)	(0.4	(0.3	(0.2	(0.1)
Lima	7.2	5.4	1.6	0.8	0.5	0.2
	(1.1)	(1.1)	(0.3	(0.2)	(0.1)	(0.1)
Coast Urban	18.4	14.1	4.1	3.0	1.4	0.9
	(2.8)	(2.3)	(0.7)	(0.6)	(0.3)	(0.2)
Coast Rural	27.0	23.5	7.9	5.8	2.9	2.0
	(4.9)	(3.4)	(1.9)	(1.1)	(0.8)	(0.5)
Sierra Urban	18.0	10.9	4.6	2.5	1.9	0.8
	(2.8)	(2.3)	(0.9)	(0.7)	(0.5)	(0.3)
Sierra Rural	29.0	24.4	8.9	5.4	4.0	1.8
	(2.2)	(2.8)	(1.0)	(0.7)	(0.6)	(0.3)
Selva Urban	13.2	10.2	2.5	2.1	0.7	0.7
	(2.6)	(1.8)	(0.6)	(0.4)	(0.2)	(0.2)
Selva Rural	33.4	25.6	9.2	5.9	3.8	2.0
	(3.8)	(3.8)	(1.6)	(1.1)	(0.9)	(0.5)

Source: Staff estimates based on ENNIV (1994, 1997).

The sensitivity tests concerned whether poverty estimates presented in the main body of the report were sensitive to household composition, size, and the poverty line chosen. In the baseline estimates presented above, we compared the *per capita* poverty line to *per capita* consumption expenditures in the different years. Although this is common practice in poverty analysis, it is important to note that a number of very stark assumptions are necessary to conduct welfare comparisons on this basis.

Equivalence Scales. The first test concerned adult equivalence scales. The food basket used in Peru was developed for a typical family of two adults and three children. In this prototype family, it was assumed that different household members have different nutritional requirements. For five members, the food basket contains about 11,900 calories for the Coast and Selva and 13,200 for the Sierra. In both cases the *per capita* requirements in the family are lower than the 2,700 calories that the World Health Organization classifies as the minimum caloric intake for an adult male.[62] Hence, in the derivation of the basic food basket, children's food requirements were given a lower importance than adult requirements.

Although the basic food basket in Peru does take the different needs of household members into account, our baseline poverty measurement does not take account household composition. This stems from the (widely applied) shortcut of deriving one general per capita (food) poverty line and applying this to all households. For example, a one-person household is measured against this per capita food poverty line and declared poor if (s)he records consumption expenditures below the treshhold - independent of the person's age or sex. Similarly, a ten-member household with nine children in it would also be measured against the (ten times) per capita poverty line, which was developed for a family of quite different characteristics. Hence, although derived from a normative concept that different people have different nutritional requirements, the way we measured poverty in this study implicitly assigns everybody an adult equivalence weight of one.

The pure way to measure poverty would assign each household in the dataset an individual poverty line that reflects the unique composition of the household. We tested to what degree our poverty comparisons are dependent on the implicit choice of an adult equivalence scale of 1.0. We did not derive a new exogenous poverty line for an adult but we conducted the following experiment: first, we chose an equivalence scale that is very different from the one in the base scenario and quite often applied in other countries: 1.0 for adults, 0.5 for children between ages 5 and 14, and 0.3 for children below age 5.[63] Second, we then chose a poverty line that results in the same percentage of the Peruvian population being poor in 1994 as when we use no adjustment for adult equivalence scales. This provides the advantage that we can control for the absolute number of poor and can now assess the impact of the adjustment on the regional distribution of poverty.

---

[62] The per capita requirements of these food baskets are high in international comparisons. The food poverty line in the Coast and Selva corresponds to 2,380 calories, in the Sierra to 2,640 calories. In most other Latin American countries, the average per capita food requirements are set at between 2,100 and 2,200 calories.

[63] See Hentschel and Lanjouw (1996) for a short discussion of adult equivalence scale ranges.

Explicit adjustment for adult equivalence scales does *not* alter the distribution of the poor or the change of poverty from 1994 to 1997 very much. Table A2.8 includes the results of the robustness test. The first two data columns show the ranking of the seven different regions with respect to the simple headcount rate - the ranking is not influenced by the introduction of adult equivalence scales (AES). The third and fourth data columns show the change in the poverty rate between 1994

Table A2.8: Adult Equivalence Scales and Poverty Rates, Peru 1994 and 1997				
	ranking w/ AES 1997	ranking w/o AES 1997	change in poverty w/AES 94-97	change in poverty w/o AES 94-97
National	-			
Lima	1	1	-9.3	-8.3
Coast Urban	4	4	-1.2	-0.5
Coast Rural	5	5	-12.0	-4.3
Sierra Urban	2	2	-14.5	-13.2
Sierra Rural	6	6	-6.1	-3.8
Selva Urban	3	3	-0.5	-0.1
Selva Rural	7	7	-7.7	-6.4

and 1997. For all regions changes go in the same direction, with the urban Sierra and Lima showing substantial gains in poverty reduction. However, the rural Coast shows a much stronger headcount reduction ratio with the adjustment for equivalence scales then without. Here, family structures changed significantly over the three years: the average household size in the poorer groups decreased, possibly due to outmigration to urban centers.

Economies of Scale. The second robustness test of our result is concerned with economies of scale in consumption. Here, we want to test the assumption that larger households have a distinct advantage over smaller households as they can benefit from sharing commodities (such as stoves, furniture, housing infrastructure) or from purchasing products in bulk, which might be cheaper. However, economies of scale in consumption would pertain to larger households independent of their age composition and are therefore quite distinct from adult equivalency, which derives from the differing needs of different household members. There is no single agreed upon method to estimate economies of scale in consumption.[64] However, to assess the importance of scale consumption, analysts often choose a value of *theta* (the degree of economies of scale) of around 0.6.[65]

In order to assess the importance of the scale effect, we conduct the following evaluation. We choose a poverty line that produces the same national poverty rate as if we were to use the unadjusted data. Having identified the subset of poor and non-poor households in both datasets, we calculate the poverty risk per household size and compare the scale-adjusted results to the non-adjusted results. These are

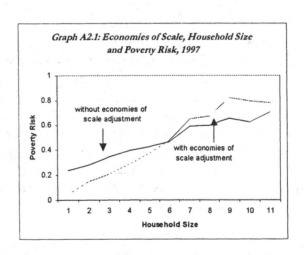

Graph A2.1: Economies of Scale, Household Size and Poverty Risk, 1997

---

[64] See Lanjouw and Ravallion (1995).

[65] This derives from the transformation of household expenditures (E) into per capita terms as $E_{pc} = E/(n^{\theta})$ where n is the household size and θ is the scale parameter. With θ equal to 1, no scale economies are assumed. The lower θ, the higher the scale effect.

portrayed in Graph A2.1. As can be seen, adjustment for economies of scale has, as expected, a flattening impact on the poverty risk/household size curve. While it remains the case that larger households have a higher likelihood of being poor, the difference in poverty rates between larger and smaller households becomes smaller. Conducting a similar analysis using the poverty gap as the welfare indicator, a very similar outcome results. We also find the relationship between the dependency ratio (the ratio of non-income earners to income-earners in the household) and household size to be robust with respect to the scale economies assumption.

Finally, we want to look at another variable that is intertwined with the above discussion: the age structure and poverty risk. Since household survey data do not permit assessment of the intra-household distribution of resources, households in their entirety are classified as poor or non-poor. Hence, if certain age groups (e.g., the elderly) are more likely to be in certain household structures (e.g., larger households), the age profile of poverty might also be influenced by scale adjustments. Graph A2.2 contains the outcomes of our estimations. We find that

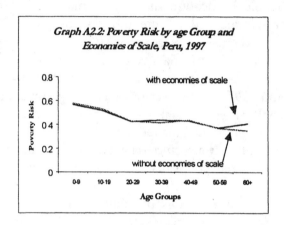

consistently in all permutations - independent of the poverty indicators looked at and whether or not we make adjustments for equivalence and economies of scale - children are the highest poverty risk group.

Distributors of World Bank Publications

Prices and credit terms vary from country to country. Consult your local distributor before placing an order.

ARGENTINA
Oficina del Libro Internacional
Av. Córdoba 1877
1120 Buenos Aires
Tel: (54 1) 815-8354
Fax: (54 1) 815-8156
E-mail: olilibro@satlink.com

AUSTRALIA, FIJI, PAPUA NEW GUINEA, SOLOMON ISLANDS, VANUATU, AND SAMOA
D.A. Information Services
648 Whitehorse Road
Mitcham 3132
Victoria
Tel: (61) 3 9210 7777
Fax: (61) 3 9210 7788
E-mail: service@dadirect.com.au

AUSTRIA
Gerold and Co.
Weihburggasse 26
A-1011 Wien
Tel: (43 1) 512-47-31-0
Fax: (43 1) 512-47-31-29

BANGLADESH
Micro Industries Development
Assistance Society (MIDAS)
House 5, Road 16
Dhanmondi R/Area
Dhaka 1209
Tel: (880 2) 326427
Fax: (880 2) 811188

BELGIUM
Jean De Lannoy
Av. du Roi 202
1060 Brussels
Tel: (32 2) 538-5169
Fax: (32 2) 538-0841

BRAZIL
Publicações Técnicas Internacionais Ltda.
Rua Peixoto Gomide, 209
01409 Sao Paulo, SP.
Tel: (55 11) 259-6644
Fax: (55 11) 258-6990
E-mail: postmaster@pti.uol.br

CANADA
Renouf Publishing Co. Ltd.
5369 Canotek Road
Ottawa, Ontario K1J 9J3
Tel: (613) 745-2665
Fax: (613) 745-7660
E-mail: order.dept@renoufbooks.com

CHINA
China Financial & Economic
Publishing House
8, Da Fo Si Dong Jie
Beijing
Tel: (86 10) 6333-8257
Fax: (86 10) 6401-7365

China Book Import Centre
P.O. Box 2825
Beijing

COLOMBIA
Infoenlace Ltda.
Carrera 6 No. 51-21
Apartado Aereo 34270
Santafé de Bogotá, D.C.
Tel: (57 1) 285-2798
Fax: (57 1) 285-2798

COTE D'IVOIRE
Center d'Edition et de Diffusion Africaines
(CEDA)
04 B.P. 541
Abidjan 04
Tel: (225) 24 6510/24 6511
Fax: (225) 25 0567

CYPRUS
Center for Applied Research
Cyprus College
6, Diogenes Street, Engomi
P.O. Box 2006
Nicosia
Tel: (357 2) 44-1730
Fax: (357 2) 46-2051

CZECH REPUBLIC
USIS, NIS Prodejna
Havelkova 22
130 00 Prague 3
Tel: (420 2) 2423 1486
Fax: (420 2) 2423 1114

DENMARK
SamfundsLitteratur
Rosenoerns Allé 11
DK-1970 Frederiksberg C
Tel: (45 31) 351942
Fax: (45 31) 357822

ECUADOR
Libri Mundi
Librería Internacional
P.O. Box 17-01-3029
Juan Leon Mera 851
Quito
Tel: (593 2) 521-606; (593 2) 544-185
Fax: (593 2) 504-209
E-mail: librimu1@librimundi.com.ec

CODEU
Ruiz de Castilla 763, Edif. Expocolor
Primer piso, Of. #2
Quito
Tel/Fax: (593 2) 507-383; 253-091
E-mail: codeu@impsat.net.ec

EGYPT, ARAB REPUBLIC OF
Al Ahram Distribution Agency
Al Galaa Street
Cairo
Tel: (20 2) 578-6083
Fax: (20 2) 578-6833

The Middle East Observer
41, Sherif Street
Cairo
Tel: (20 2) 393-9732
Fax: (20 2) 393-9732

FINLAND
Akateeminen Kirjakauppa
P.O. Box 128
FIN-00101 Helsinki
Tel: (358 0) 121 4418
Fax: (358 0) 121-4435
E-mail: akatilaus@stockmann.fi

FRANCE
World Bank Publications
66, avenue d'Iéna
75116 Paris
Tel: (33 1) 40-69-30-56/57
Fax: (33 1) 40-69-30-68

GERMANY
UNO-Verlag
Poppelsdorfer Allee 55
53115 Bonn
Tel: (49 228) 949020
Fax: (49 228) 217492
E-mail: unoverlag@aol.com

GHANA
Epp Books Services
P.O. Box 44
TUC
Accra

GREECE
Papasotiriou S.A.
35, Stournara Str.
106 82 Athens
Tel: (30 1) 364-1826
Fax: (30 1) 364-8254

HAITI
Culture Diffusion
5, Rue Capois
C.P. 257
Port-au-Prince
Tel: (509) 23 9260
Fax: (509) 23 4858

HONG KONG, CHINA; MACAO
Asia 2000 Ltd.
Sales & Circulation Department
Seabird House, unit 1101-02
22-28 Wyndham Street, Central
Hong Kong
Tel: (852) 2530-1409
Fax: (852) 2526-1107
E-mail: sales@asia2000.com.hk

HUNGARY
Euro Info Service
Margitszgeti Europa Haz
H-1138 Budapest
Tel: (36 1) 350 80 24, 350 80 25
Fax: (36 1) 350 90 32
E-mail: euroinfo@mail.matav.hu

INDIA
Allied Publishers Ltd.
751 Mount Road
Madras - 600 002
Tel: (91 44) 852-3938
Fax: (91 44) 852-0649

INDONESIA
Pt. Indira Limited
Jalan Borobudur 20
P.O. Box 181
Jakarta 10320
Tel: (62 21) 390-4290
Fax: (62 21) 390-4289

IRAN
Ketab Sara Co. Publishers
Khaled Eslamboli Ave., 6th Street
Delafrooz Alley No. 8
P.O. Box 15745-733
Tehran 15117
Tel: (98 21) 8717819; 8716104
Fax: (98 21) 8712479
E-mail: ketab-sara@neda.net.ir

Kowkab Publishers
P.O. Box 19575-511
Tehran
Tel: (98 21) 258-3723
Fax: (98 21) 258-3723

IRELAND
Government Supplies Agency
Oifig an tSoláthair
4-5 Harcourt Road
Dublin 2
Tel: (353 1) 661-3111
Fax: (353 1) 475-2670

ISRAEL
Yozmot Literature Ltd.
P.O. Box 56055
3 Yohanan Hasandlar Street
Tel Aviv 61560
Tel: (972 3) 5285-397
Fax: (972 3) 5285-397

R.O.Y. International
PO Box 13056
Tel Aviv 61130
Tel: (972 3) 5461423
Fax: (972 3) 5461442
E-mail: royil@netvision.net.il

Palestinian Authority/Middle East
Index Information Services
P.O.B. 19502 Jerusalem
Tel: (972 2) 6271219
Fax: (972 2) 6271634

ITALY
Licosa Commissionaria Sansoni SPA
Via Duca Di Calabria, 1/1
Casella Postale 552
50125 Firenze
Tel: (55) 645-415
Fax: (55) 641-257
E-mail: licosa@ftbcc.it

JAMAICA
Ian Randle Publishers Ltd.
206 Old Hope Road, Kingston 6
Tel: 876-927-2085
Fax: 876-977-0243
E-mail: irpl@colis.com

JAPAN
Eastern Book Service
3-13 Hongo 3-chome, Bunkyo-ku
Tokyo 113
Tel: (81 3) 3818-0861
Fax: (81 3) 3818-0864
E-mail: orders@svt-ebs.co.jp

KENYA
Africa Book Service (E.A.) Ltd.
Quaran House, Mfangano Street
P.O. Box 45245
Nairobi
Tel: (254 2) 223 641
Fax: (254 2) 330 272

KOREA, REPUBLIC OF
Daejon Trading Co. Ltd.
P.O. Box 34, Youida, 706 Seoun Bldg
44-6 Youido-Dong, Yeongchengpo-Ku
Seoul
Tel: (82 2) 785-1631/4
Fax: (82 2) 784-0315

LEBANON
Librairie du Liban
P.O. Box 11-9232
Beirut
Tel: (961 9) 217 944
Fax: (961 9) 217 434

MALAYSIA
University of Malaya Cooperative
Bookshop, Limited
P.O. Box 1127
Jalan Pantai Baru
59700 Kuala Lumpur
Tel: (60 3) 756-5000
Fax: (60 3) 755-4424
E-mail: umkoop@tm.net.my

MEXICO
INFOTEC
Av. San Fernando No. 37
Col. Toriello Guerra
14050 Mexico, D.F.
Tel: (52 5) 624-2800
Fax: (52 5) 624-2822
E-mail: infotec@rtn.net.mx

Mundi-Prensa Mexico S.A. de C.V.
c/Rio Panuco, 141-Colonia Cuauhtemoc
06500 Mexico, D.F.
Tel: (52 5) 533-5658
Fax: (52 5) 514-6799

NEPAL
Everest Media International Services (P) Ltd.
GPO Box 5443
Kathmandu
Tel: (977 1) 472 152
Fax: (977 1) 224 431

NETHERLANDS
De Lindeboom/InOr-Publikaties
P.O. Box 202, 7480 AE Haaksbergen
Tel: (31 53) 574-0004
Fax: (31 53) 572-9296
E-mail: lindeboo@worldonline.nl

NEW ZEALAND
EBSCO NZ Ltd.
Private Mail Bag 99914
New Market
Auckland
Tel: (64 9) 524-8119
Fax: (64 9) 524-8067

NIGERIA
University Press Limited
Three Crowns Building Jericho
Private Mail Bag 5095
Ibadan
Tel: (234 22) 41-1356
Fax: (234 22) 41-2056

NORWAY
NIC Info A/S
Book Department, Postboks 6512 Etterstad
N-0606 Oslo
Tel: (47 22) 97-4500
Fax: (47 22) 97-4545

PAKISTAN
Mirza Book Agency
65, Shahrah-e-Quaid-e-Azam
Lahore 54000
Tel: (92 42) 735 3601
Fax: (92 42) 576 3714

Oxford University Press
5 Bangalore Town
Sharae Faisal
Karachi-75350
Tel: (92 21) 446307
Fax: (92 21) 4547640

Pak Book Corporation
Aziz Chambers 21, Queen's Road
Lahore
Tel: (92 42) 636 3222; 636 0885
Fax: (92 42) 636 2328

PERU
Editorial Desarrollo SA
Apartado 3824, Lima 1
Tel: (51 14) 285380
Fax: (51 14) 286628

PHILIPPINES
International Booksource Center Inc.
1127-A Antipolo St, Barangka, Venezuela
Makati City
Tel: (63 2) 896 6501; 6505; 6507
Fax: (63 2) 896 1741

POLAND
International Publishing Service
Ul. Piekna 31/37
00-677 Warzawa
Tel: (48 2) 628-6089
Fax: (48 2) 621-7255
E-mail: books%ips@ikp.atm.com.pl

PORTUGAL
Livraria Portugal
Apartado 2681, Rua Do Carmo 70-74
1200 Lisbon
Tel: (1) 347-4982
Fax: (1) 347-0264

ROMANIA
Compani De Librarii Bucuresti S.A.
Str. Lipscani no. 26, sector 3
Bucharest
Tel: (40 1) 613 9645
Fax: (40 1) 312 4000

RUSSIAN FEDERATION
Isdatelstvo <Ves Mir>
9a, Kolpachniy Pereulok
Moscow 101831
Tel: (7 095) 917 87 49
Fax: (7 095) 917 92 59

SINGAPORE; TAIWAN, CHINA; MYANMAR; BRUNEI
Ashgate Publishing Asia Pacific Pte. Ltd.
41 Kallang Pudding Road #04-03
Golden Wheel Building
Singapore 349316
Tel: (65) 741-5166
Fax: (65) 742-9356
E-mail: ashgate@asianconnect.com

SLOVENIA
Gospodarski Vestnik Publishing Group
Dunajska cesta 5
1000 Ljubljana
Tel: (386 61) 133 83 47; 132 12 30
Fax: (386 61) 133 80 30
E-mail: repansekj@gvestnik.si

SOUTH AFRICA, BOTSWANA
For single titles:
Oxford University Press Southern Africa
Vasco Boulevard, Goodwood
P.O. Box 12119, N1 City 7463
Cape Town
Tel: (27 21) 595 4400
Fax: (27 21) 595 4430
E-mail: oxford@oup.co.za

For subscription orders:
International Subscription Service
P.O. Box 41095
Craighall
Johannesburg 2024
Tel: (27 11) 880-1448
Fax: (27 11) 880-6248
E-mail: iss@is.co.za

SPAIN
Mundi-Prensa Libros, S.A.
Castello 37
28001 Madrid
Tel: (34 1) 431-3399
Fax: (34 1) 575-3998
E-mail: libreria@mundiprensa.es

Mundi-Prensa Barcelona
Consell de Cent, 391
08009 Barcelona
Tel: (34 3) 488-3492
Fax: (34 3) 487-7659
E-mail: barcelona@mundiprensa.es

SRI LANKA, THE MALDIVES
Lake House Bookshop
100, Sir Chittampalam Gardiner Mawatha
Colombo 2
Tel: (94 1) 32105

Fax: (94 1) 432104
E-mail: LHL@sri.lanka.net

SWEDEN
Wennergren-Williams AB
P.O. Box 1305
S-171 25 Solna
Tel: (46 8) 705-97-50
Fax: (46 8) 27-00-71
E-mail: mail@wwi.se

SWITZERLAND
Librairie Payot Service Institutionnel
Côtes-de-Montbenon 30
1002 Lausanne
Tel: (41 21) 341-3229
Fax: (41 21) 341-3235

ADECO Van Diermen EditionsTechniques
Ch. de Lacuez 41
CH1807 Blonay
Tel: (41 21) 943 2673
Fax: (41 21) 943 3605

THAILAND
Central Books Distribution
306 Silom Road
Bangkok 10500
Tel: (66 2) 235-5400
Fax: (66 2) 237-8321

TRINIDAD & TOBAGO AND THE CARRIBBEAN
Systematics Studies Ltd.
St. Augustine Shopping Center
Eastern Main Road, St. Augustine
Trinidad & Tobago, West Indies
Tel: (868) 645-8466
Fax: (868) 645-8467
E-mail: tobe@trinidad.net

UGANDA
Gustro Ltd.
PO Box 9997, Madhvani Building
Plot 16/4 Jinja Rd.
Kampala
Tel: (256 41) 251 467
Fax: (256 41) 251 468
E-mail: gus@swiftuganda.com

UNITED KINGDOM
Microinfo Ltd.
P.O. Box 3, Alton, Hampshire GU34 2PG
England
Tel: (44 1420) 86848
Fax: (44 1420) 89889
E-mail: wbank@ukminfo.demon.co.uk

The Stationery Office
51 Nine Elms Lane
London SW8 5DR
Tel: (44 171) 873-8400
Fax: (44 171) 873-8242

VENEZUELA
Tecni-Ciencia Libros, S.A.
Centro Cuidad Comercial Tamanco
Nivel C2, Caracas
Tel: (58 2) 959 5547; 5035; 0016
Fax: (58 2) 959 5636

ZAMBIA
University Bookshop, University of Zambia
Great East Road Campus
P.O. Box 32379
Lusaka
Tel: (260 1) 252 576
Fax: (260 1) 253 952

ZIMBABWE
Academic and Baobab Books (Pvt.) Ltd.
4 Conald Road, Graniteside
P.O. Box 567
Harare
Tel: 263 4 755035
Fax: 263 4 781913

DATE DUE

ILL7588724		